TURNAROUND PRINCIPALS FOR UNDERPERFORMING SCHOOLS

Rosemary Papa
Fenwick English

ROWMAN & LITTLEFIELD EDUCATION

A division of
ROWMAN & LITTLEFIELD PUBLISHERS, INC.
Lanham • New York • Toronto • Plymouth, UK

Published by Rowman & Littlefield Education
A division of Rowman & Littlefield Publishers, Inc.
A wholly owned subsidiary of The Rowman & Littlefield Publishing Group, Inc.
4501 Forbes Boulevard, Suite 200, Lanham, Maryland 20706
http://www.rowmaneducation.com

Estover Road, Plymouth PL6 7PY, United Kingdom

British Library Cataloguing in Publication Information Available

Library of Congress Cataloging-in-Publication Data

Papa, Rosemary.
  Turnaround principals for underperforming schools / Rosemary Papa and
Fenwick W. English.
     p. cm.
  Includes index.
  ISBN 978-1-60709-972-7 (cloth : alk. paper) — ISBN 978-1-60709-973-4 (pbk.
: alk. paper) — ISBN 978-1-60709-974-1 (electronic)
  1. School improvement programs. 2. School principals. I. English, Fenwick
W. II. Title. III. Title: Turn around principals for underperforming schools.
  LB2822.8.P37 2011
  371.2'07—dc22

                                                           2011014625

Printed in the United States of America

We dedicate this book to
those professional practitioners,
administrators, and teachers in
the public schools who still live and
work there in the cause of social justice
for a better society and world
and who are "called" to this mission.

CONTENTS

CONTENTS

ACKNOWLEDGMENTS

We acknowledge all of those friends and colleagues who took time to listen and encourage us over the years, and even our critics who also took us seriously and to whom we owe more than we knew at the time.

And especially Josie, Dominic, and Maggie, for whom public schools are and should remain caring and safe places to be.

FOREWORD

Try a thought experiment. Before you read further, let me invite you to stop a moment and think about what you believe to be the essence of a school in need of a "turnaround" principal. Come up with two or three features of these schools, and then return to reading. This is what I did prior to reading the book you have in hand, and it's a fruitful way to begin.

If you're like me, you may have struggled a little with the notion of a turnaround school. To say a school needs to turn around, you have to assume that it's really going in the wrong direction.

And for schools to be going in the wrong direction, these are some of the features one would expect: students are not happy; adults are not happy; students are failing to learn; families are not involved; test scores are probably miserable; the environment is uninviting, maybe even scary or unsafe; the tone of the place is either critical or uncaring, and that goes for youngsters and adults; the reputation of the school serves to send people away rather than attract them; ultimately, the school chokes off opportunities instead of engendering them.

In short, imagine the features we hope from our best schools, conjure up the binary opposites, and then you have a school that needs a "turnaround" principal.

Of course, there are still problems. For one thing, I think it's fairly safe to say that no one—absolutely no one—sets out to create a school as miserable as the products we've imagined. No professional walks into it with pride and a sense of self-satisfaction, not even a lazy devotee of mediocrity. There is no intent to create the institution as fiasco. But more importantly, look back at your list—or mine, if you cheated—and identify how many of these items can be "fixed" by the "turnaround" principal, or anyone else short of Superman.

It turns out that turning around is not just a task for the superhero; it's a project for the community. Who can help those adults and children embrace the joy of learning and the sense of purpose that makes coming together important? What if the core issue in the discontent of the students has more to do with what's not in their stomachs and what's not in their after-school world than what's not in their school day?

What if the miserable haven of the school building merely reflects even more miserable conditions in the neighborhood? Who doesn't put learning low on the list when life's basic needs are unmet or when there is a crisis to solve?

So, one might ask, in the midst of all this excuse-making from me, is there a place for the "turnaround" principal? I believe there is, and I further believe that Papa and English have woven a tapestry of qualities that can help us not only understand the kind of person who might help gather the forces that can turn around the site of failed learning, but also help us to nurture those qualities in our leaders.

Note the language in the last paragraph. I am reluctant to say that schools need to be turned around, at least in the larger context. There are certainly schools that have harbored ineffective educators and passed on a legacy of failure for their students. These are exactly the sorts of institutions that need help in the form of someone willing to disrupt the comfort of carrying on in dysfunction.

But what image of that disruptor do we want to promote? I recall the dominant image of the turnaround act from my own television-tainted imagination: the stagecoach careening through twisting mountain trails, headed inexorably toward the cliff, the horses mad with fear. Into this treacherous dash, the fearless cowboy (wholly other and from the outside) leaps on the lead horses, grappling with the pounding of hooves and the dust of the trails and the determined, sweaty gallop to certain death, halting them just steps before the precipice to turn them around and save the day. Turn around!

I don't know that Papa and English share my concern about transferring the underlying assumptions of the language related to "turnaround" schools and principals, but they surely share the concern of oversimplification. There appears to be a popular myth that the prescription for weak schools is about as simple and dramatic as stopping the stagecoach—as long as you have that "cowboy" coming in from the outside.

In contrast to this simplification, Papa and English help us understand the task faced by leaders in troubled schools in a completely different manner. Creating a high-performing school, they remind us, is always a "dynamic combination of leadership and circumstance embedded in specific contexts." The locus for change is not just in an aberrant school, and the solution is not a go-it-alone leader.

Rather, the key issue relates to social justice, and a leader who can bring together constituents in a participatory effort. Sensitive to the context, leaders pay attention to the teaching that goes on in the schools, but also the community conditions that give rise to despair or even a legitimate form of resistance, as well as the system in which any given troubled school is situated.

Acknowledging that school leaders generally have a systematic preparation in the "basics" of leadership, the text relies instead on what Papa and English refer to as "heuristics" of leadership. Integrated with careful discussion of big ideas such as the context of schools, the blend of theory and action, and a profound commitment to schools as promoters of social justice, heuristics of leadership provide reflective milestones for the aspiring leader.

These heuristics offer developing leaders a means to align their skills and knowledge with a set of values and actions that promise to serve both the children and the adults in troubled schools, as well as the communities that foster such schools.

One of the teachers quoted in the introduction to chapter 3 says, "We don't teach in failing schools. We teach in failing communities." The vision for a turnaround principal doesn't promise to halt the stagecoach just in time; rather, this vision of a turnaround principal is truly one who *turns around* in order to see the full complexity of a school's situation, so that, uniting the efforts of teachers, students, and community members, a school can become the place we all really want to begin with: a place where learning is honored in a caring environment.

Daniel L. Kain
Professor of Education
Vice Provost for Academic Personnel
Northern Arizona University

1

TAKING THE MYSTERY OUT OF TURNING AROUND UNDERPERFORMING AND FAILING SCHOOLS

We'll do whatever is necessary to do a good job.

—urban public school principal,
From Papa & Fortune, 2002

I can't just be a paper pusher and sit in my office. My vision has to be their vision. Principals have to be service-oriented and know the reading, math, and curriculum. I am in the classroom and visible in the school.

—urban public school principal

Underperforming or failing schools are not hard to identify. A simple question to parents, community leaders, and students reveals that there is no issue in recognizing which schools are performing and which are not. The evidence is all around and is not confined to merely test scores published in the local paper or listening to real estate agents extol why property values in one area of a school district are high and others are much lower.

The myth that increased testing is required to know where schools are working and where they are not is just that: a myth.

Tests may reveal the specific gaps in academic achievement but underperformance is recognizable long before that.

High-performing schools have the earmarks of success at all levels: academics, athletics, extracurricular activities, and social events. Students in high-performing schools talk of teachers who care, administrators whom they know and who talk to them, and strong student esprit de corps as marked by good attendance in class, at games, and at social gatherings.

A high-performing school is not simply an academic test prep factory, but an organic whole. Such schools are vibrant, nurturing, and warm, coupled with high expectations for the development of the whole human being as an intellectual, artistic, humane social person who understands the essence of democratic participation and citizenship.

The research reported in this book was and is a continuing attempt to deconstruct the obvious status of high-performing schools to unlock the attributes and practices going on within them. And while that research has consistently revealed the elements of what makes a school high performing, it similarly provides no magic formula or silver bullet.

High-performing schools cannot be reduced to soup recipes. We learned that with the so-called "effective schools" research. In that approach we found that while there were common elements of effective schools and that these elements were correlative, they were not predictive; that is, simply putting them together in a mixing bowl did not produce the same salad (English, 1994, p. 51; 2002).

The simple fact is this: the creation of a high-performing school is always a dynamic combination of leadership and circumstance embedded in specific contexts. While it is true that leaders do certain things, the recitation of those things offers no guarantee that the results will be the same from place to place.

On the other side of this situation we can say this: without knowledgeable leadership nothing much will happen. We say "knowledgeable" leadership because it goes beyond just a commitment to "do better" or "work harder." There are plenty of low-performing or failing schools in which the leaders work hard or are simply committed to making those schools better. To transform a low-performing school into a high-performing one surely and obviously takes commitment and hard work, but beyond that it takes knowledge of *what to do, how to do it, and the courage to act.*

This book is about shedding light on what leaders do, which is a derivative of the empirical work undertaken in 2002 (Papa & Fortune) and updated in 2011 (Papa, 2010) as well as empirical work on educational administrative heuristics reported in a broad array of national and international research journals and books undertaken by English and Bolton (2008) and Bolton and English (2009; 2010a, 2010b).

A VIEW OF LEADERSHIP: LONE RANGERS DON'T MAKE IT

There are so many half-truths and simplicities about leadership in the marketplace today that we have to take a deep breath before once again taking up the subject. We eschew the "kitsch management books" which litter airport book shops and which proffer the—put in any word you would like here—"seven [*ten, twelve, most important*] effective [*successful, key*] habits [*secrets, mistakes, laws*] of leading organizations or groups" (English, 2008, pp. 160–66; Papa, Kain & Brown, in press; Samier, 2005).

Most of these texts are common-sense observations. These texts then are turned into universal bromides which erase context.

Such an erasure also removes the power of prediction. Leadership success is far more complex and nuanced than these "quickies" proffer. Kitsch books promise simplistic Alka-Seltzer remedies and happy endings. Our research indicates that no such promises can be made, and that without continued maintenance efforts, even high-performing schools can slip. Once high-performing, not always high-performing! The bad news is that there is no permanent status for excellence. The good news is that low-performing schools can become better. So it works both ways.

We begin with an observation of major change in the U.S. undertaken by Anyon (2005), who indicated that solitary leaders do not bring about major changes. Rather as Thomson (2008) in the United Kingdom observed about school principals (called *headteachers* there):

> Even small-scale reforms are produced through a complex interplay of scales, actors, histories and ideologies, in which the vast majority of policy actors are collectives. From this perspective, it seems relatively unproductive for leadership/management scholars to simply look at the actions of individual headteachers for evidence of resistance to and critique of policy agendas, and imperative to look to their collective activities. (p. 93)

Our research supports these perspectives. Leaders who turn around low-performing or failing schools cannot do it alone and never do it alone. School leadership is about collective actions by a multitude of players and policy actors. Leadership is about working with and through lots of people, not only in the actual schools but in off-school sites as well: central office administrators, parents, social workers, law enforcement personnel, welfare and related medical/ mental health staff, and more.

Leaders both initiate and respond. Sometimes they even react. Leaders are catalysts. Leaders provide meaning to hard work. Leaders tie activities together. Leaders provide consensus and continuity. Leaders are problem-solvers and puzzle-unpackers.

Leaders do what they do by "being there." They are witnesses and provocateurs. Their mere presence is affirming. This is the story behind the story. In the end, leadership is performance. It is a form of public theatre and the end result is to build strong collectivities within and without the schools which will change their directions and practices and initiate a continuing cycle of reflection and subsequent improvement over many years.

THE LENS OF PERFORMATIVITY: TWO VIEWS OF THINKING ABOUT TURNING SCHOOLS AROUND

Schools exist in an intricate web of functions and relationships to powerful sociopolitical agencies. Any particular school in the U.S. usually has a relationship to the larger school system which may also have a legal or fiduciary connection to a county governmental body for budgetary support or oversight, state departments of education and other state regulatory agencies such as health, and finally to the federal government. Any specific school sends its graduates to other schools or to the world of work if their students are of age to work.

These connections exert pressures and influences and often impose regulations and restrictions, some of which may have little to do with education. It is not with fond memories that we remember having to take down student papers and artwork put up in the hallways by order of the local fire chief who could not care less about motivating student learning by displaying outstanding academic or artistic educational results.

How an educational leader views the matter of student performance and ultimately school performance will say much about what is done and how what is done is interpreted not only by those working and living in a school, but by all of the other connections which impinge on it through those related agencies.

Table 1.1 shows two views of performativity. They have been derived, adapted, and expanded from the work of Helen Gunter (2002, pp. 18–19). These two views are simply entitled *Lens 1* and *Lens 2*. There are six areas of performativity as shown in Table 1.1.

About Lens 1: The Ideology of Neo-Liberalism

Lens 1 is called *neo-liberalism*. Neo-liberalism is a loosely held set of beliefs that has permeated the public sector for several decades, promoted by right-wing think tanks sponsored by some of the most

Table 1.1. Two Views of School Performativity

Lens 1	Aspect	Lens 2
Education is a commodified service to be subjected to the forces of a competitive marketplace to satisfy "customers" on demand.	The Nature of Education	Education is a public service, a social guarantee of an entitlement for all children to promote opportunity, equality, and equity.
The purpose of schools is to prepare workers to be skilled to keep the nation competitive in the international business marketplace.	The Purpose of Schools	The purpose of schools is to prepare citizens to function in a democracy that works to progressively expand the benefits of a free society to everyone, especially the most marginalized.
Leadership revolves around embracing entrepreneurial behaviors and activities that produce winners and losers and perpetuate the current socioeconomic-political structure which keeps them in place.	The Nature of Leadership	Leadership is a collaborative enterprise to produce greater opportunities to embrace civic humanism and reduce socioeconomic disparities which schools perpetuate.
Accountability is aimed at identifying stragglers, non-believers, skeptics, and critics who are opposed to commodifying education via strict adherence to test scores. Tests are used to control and punish.	Accountability	Accountability is about producing more opportunities to celebrate difference and to become more inclusive as opposed to exclusive. Tests are only one measure and are not perfect barometers of improved performance.
The role of management is to exercise tight control over all system functions and to require compliance and greater surveillance of all activities.	Nature of Management	The role of management is to expand and differentiate forms of pedagogy and to support creative teaching.
There is no role for social justice in this view; it is superfluous because it contradicts individual choice. The lack of social justice is then blamed on individuals making poor choices in the marketplace.	Social Justice	Social justice is a major goal of this view, sought through equalizing opportunity for advancement in the larger society and the role of the school in that society.

politically conservative and regressive forces in the larger society. Neo-liberalism has been defined by Harvey (2009) as

> a theory of political economic practices that proposes that human well-being can best be advanced by liberating individual entrepreneurial freedoms and skills within an institutional framework characterized by strong private property rights, free markets, and free trade. The role of the state is to create and preserve an institutional framework appropriate to such practices. (p. 2)

An ideology is defined as "a closed system of beliefs or values in which the original assumptions of those beliefs or values are never questioned but accepted as 'givens'" (English, 2010, p. 130).

Neo-liberals have a fanaticism attached to the ideology of the free market, an ideology that "the social good will be maximized by maximizing the reach and frequency of market transactions, and it seeks to bring all human action into the domain of the market" (Harvey, 2009, p. 3). The success of neo-liberalism is that its tenets have been pushed as a form of "common sense" about things when in reality it is simply a form of constructed self-interest masquerading under the banner of individual liberty.

The idea that no form of government should be allowed to constrain a free market espoused in the "efficient market hypothesis" is responsible for the worldwide financial collapse in which huge banks which were undercapitalized went under and massive amounts of public funds were required as fiduciary life-savers.

As Fox (2009) observed, the "efficient market hypothesis" was a "scientific construct, a model for understanding [and] not to be taken as a literal description of reality [because] all scientific models are oversimplifications" (p. xiv). Perhaps the greatest flaw of the "efficient market hypothesis" was the assumption that the market was rational in the first place.

However, rationality and data-driven decision making as the sole arbitrators of administrative action are the tools of corporate management. With such tools in hand it isn't necessary for the leaders to be educators at all. They can be managers from anywhere (Thomas B. Fordham Institute and Broad Foundation, 2003).

The neo-liberal agenda was most forcefully advanced by Lewis Powell, before he joined the U.S. Supreme Court, in a famous confidential memo to the United States Chamber of Commerce in 1971 in which he advocated that the Chamber "should lead an assault upon the major institutions—universities, schools, the media, publishing, the courts—in order to change how individuals think" about private enterprise, culture and corporate activities (Harvey, 2009, p. 43).

The U.S. Chamber and the Business Round Table have become prime movers of the neo-liberal agenda in education, pushing increased standardization, more and more testing, merit pay, and the privatization of schooling (Apple, 2006; Emery & Ohanian, 2004; Giroux, 2004; Ravitch, 2010).

A "turnaround" school from *Lens 1* would mean that "success" is defined with principals and/or non-educators who run schools with ruthlessness and a single-minded agenda aimed at getting higher test scores. These principals and/or non-educators have no interest in pursuing the role of schools as agents of social reproduction, which actually increases the distance between the haves and the have-nots in the larger social order.

Schools are not places where there is serious questioning permitted of that social order and where parents are considered "customers" who are enabled to "shop around" for good schools. In this scenario the state is relieved of any responsibility to provide good schools for the poor and disenfranchised elements of our society. "If the schools are poor it's because bad choices were made by them" (Barry, 2007, p. 159). The only role for the state is to ensure that such choices exist. Thus, neo-liberalism attacks policies which impact the most vulnerable part of the socioeconomic population spectrum.

Lens 1 has no place for social justice issues or leaders concerned about them. This lens views diversity as a "dilemma" or a "problem" to be overcome. The approach is to make all students the same, which means "white euro-Americans, upper middle class and suburban" (Marshall & Parker, 2006, p. 195). And as Marshall & Parker

(2006) similarly observe, "The tradition of schooling for assimilation, making all students and learners the same, undermines social justice efforts" (p. 195).

Wiens (2006) observed this about *Lens 1*:

> It dawned on us that the language of reform was not primarily about and centrally about education. Rather, it was about economic ideology, sometimes called "the business agenda"—full of phrases like economic advantage, competition, customer satisfaction, consumers, products, stakeholders, entrepreneurship, human resources, and the like . . . any serious notions of education seemed absent from the debate. (p. 216)

We do not see the turning around of low-performing or failing schools as fulfilling the need to restore the nation's competitive position in the world's economy. We see it, rather, as a fulfillment of the nation's most cherished ideals for the dignity and worth of every human being's fulfillment and promise for respect. Indeed, in pursuing and "turning around" low-performing schools we eschew the "business agenda" and any further corporatization of American public education.

The "business agenda" and neo-liberal mind-set are already making an inroad among the leadership at the college level. As the number of non-academics leading colleges has begun to increase, Ekman (2010) noted:

> We should be concerned that a growing number of colleges are being led by people who have never had direct experience in the heart of the enterprise as faculty members, department chairs, deans, or provosts. If the number continues to increase, the risk is that higher education will become an industry that is led by people who do not truly understand it, who view it as a commodity to be traded, a production problem to be solved efficiently, or a brand to be marketed. (p. A88)

We see the same problem in spades at the elementary and secondary school level with the passage of policies, regulations, and laws such as No Child Left Behind and the present administration's Race to the Top. It can also be seen with the recent appointment of non-educators to some urban superintendencies.

Most recently, the issue was seen with the appointment and recent firing of Cathleen Black to New York City's educational system as chancellor of its public schools by Mayor Bloomberg, a millionaire businessman. She lasted only a few months (Martinez & Saul, 2001, April 8). Ms. Black had no previous experience in teaching or administering public schools. She is a former magazine magnate and member of the board of directors of Coca Cola (Anderson, November, 2010).

About Lens 2: The Perspective of Social Justice and Schools for Democracy

A "turnaround" school from the view of *Lens 2* would envision education as a public good. It is a school for all children which fundamentally reaches into "the deep roots of injustice emanating from competitive market forces, economic policies, political practices, and traditions that maintain elite privilege" (Marshall & Oliva, 2006, p. 5).

"Turnaround" schools within *Lens 2* see the role of management as expanding forms of pedagogy and supporting creative teaching and emphasizing active learning. Leadership within *Lens 2* is seen as a collaborative enterprise to promote greater opportunities and wider definitions of success, and it envisions the purpose of schools as preparing citizens to function in a democratic environment.

We proffer our definition of *social justice* as: schooling that recognizes and respects the fundamental differences in cultural identity and social experiences that place some children and their families at the margins of American culture and society, and which is aimed at removing such barriers which keep them there—not by assimilation (which is social silencing and erasure), but by working to remove the barriers, techniques, beliefs, and practices which put them there in the first place.

And most fundamental of all is the challenging of the doctrine of social conservatism in all its forms, which sees schools as reproductive agents of the socioeconomic status quo.

These two views or lenses regarding the purpose of education, schooling, accountability, and the nature of leadership position the research undertaken in this book and provide meaning for the discussion which follows.

RESULTS PRESENTED AS HEURISTICS FOR DECISION MAKING

Throughout this book we will present our observations and recommendations based on the research reported as *heuristics*: involving or serving as an aid to learning, discovery, or problem-solving by experimental means and especially by trial and error (Merriam-Webster, 2010, p. 1).

Davis (2004) indicated that thinking heuristically enabled a decision maker to cut problems into smaller pieces by "chunking patterns of information" into *rules of thumb*. By this term Davis meant that information "is organized mentally via predetermined metarules that are category based and whole pattern in structure" (p. 631).

The approach has been supported by research conducted by Nestor-Baker and Hoy in 2001 when they discerned in a study of forty-four Ohio school superintendents that such chunking was a key feature in job success. They summarized their study by saying that "the reputationally successful [superintendents]—those who can be considered as expert performers—have larger amounts of *if-then* scenarios to draw on in navigating the superintendency, allowing them a seemingly intuitive orientation to the tasks at hand" (p. 123).

One of the research findings on administrative decision making in the U.S. and the U.K. by English and Bolton (2008) found that

> emotions and feelings were always present in the locus of decision re-
> counted by those interviewed. . . . Decision makers did not think first
> and feel second. Rather, they were constantly feeling emotions and so
> learned to recognize the signs of their feelings, especially when they
> became aware that a decision may be wrong or inappropriate. (p. 104)

We will say more about this shortly.

Previous Research about Turnaround Schools

Of particular importance to this initial discussion regarding turn-around schools is previous research reported by the WWC or What Works Clearinghouse (Institute of Education Sciences-IES, 2008) which, ". . . using a semi-structured hierarchy classification created by IES to determine the strength of the evidence based grounding" (p. 1), identified three levels of classification.

A strong level of evidence was determined by randomized control trials. A moderate level of evidence used quasi-experimental or cor-relational research. The final, low level, focused on expert opinion, derived from strong findings or theories in related areas.

WWC defined turnaround schools as schools that met two criteria:

- They began as chronically poor performers—with a high pro-portion of their students (generally 20 percent or more) failing to meet state standards of proficiency in mathematics or read-ing as defined under No Child Left Behind over two or more consecutive years.
- They showed substantial gains in student achievement in a short time (no more than three years). Examples of substan-tial gains in achievement are reducing by at least 10 percent-age points the proportion of students failing to meet state standards for proficiency in mathematics or reading, showing similarly large improvements in other measures of academic

performance (such as lowering the dropout rate by 10 percentage points or more), or improving overall performance on standardized mathematics or reading tests by an average of 10 percentage points (or about 0.25 standard deviations).

The schools reported in this book met these criteria, according to the data reported in the studies (Institute of Education Sciences-IES, 2008, pp. 4–5).

A total of thirty-five schools were identified in the WWC study. They were: twenty-one elementary schools, eight middle schools, and six high schools.

The heuristics presented in this revised book were based on ten case studies derived from these thirty-five school studies that examined turnaround practices. The WWC data indicated the following practices, or what we are labeling "heuristics" or themes identified through trial-and-error research, are involved in turning around low-performing schools:

Heuristic 1: A dramatic change should be signaled (low evidence). The data from the WWC indicated that there has to be a signal of some sort that things are not going to be the same as before, an important sign to those inside and outside the school that a significant break or interruption is going to occur. What this means is that awareness has to be created that it's not going to be "business as usual" any longer. There is no one "best way" to signal such a change. The means should fit the context, however. And the "fit" is not a matter of science, but one of "art."

Heuristic 2: A consistent focus on instruction (low evidence). The key to turning around a low-performing school is to focus on instruction. The reason is not hard to discern. Student performance is normally determined by test scores because they are the cheapest means to define performance. One must know how "low performance" is defined before attempting to organize the energies of the people inside and outside of a school site. Differentiating instruction and making sure it is aligned to the means of measurement is usually a key element in engaging in "improvement" (English, 2010).

Heuristic 3: Select improvements that are visible and easiest to secure (low evidence). There are many means to securing school improvement. Heuristic 2 indicated that they should be focused on instruction. This heuristic requires the school leader and staff to sort through and make those improvements which have the best chance of making an impact very early in the process.

Early wins provide confidence both to those inside the school and to constituents and even critics that better times are on the way. To do this requires some sophistication in understanding what the factors and variables are in supporting the entire instructional/curricula process.

Simplistic business models are usually ignorant of the core of the educational enterprise. Business models are about management and not about instruction, except perhaps to search for ways to reduce costs and improve efficiencies. It is possible to have a well-managed school and low student achievement. One does not usually imply the other. However, if a school is poorly managed overall, that usually includes the instructional program, and hence the appearance is that if managerial techniques are installed to create order, this will somehow improve instructional performance as well.

Heuristic 4: Build a committed staff (low evidence). The key to leadership in turning low-performing schools around is that there has to be a "critical mass" of like-minded professionals and support staff that are committed to improvement. While we think that the word "culture" is often overused for schools—as is "climate"—there has to be a concerted effort toward creating a sense of palpable expectations for change which requires concerted work toward change and toward advancement. The school leader works *with and through people*.

The ability of the principal to connect with and excite teachers and staff and to convince mostly by example is pivotal in school improvement. The principal has to be "out front" but can't be the only one "in front." Finding ways for many people to shine is key. The old saying "It's amazing how much can be accomplished if one is not worried about who gets the credit" epitomizes the posture of the school leader.

We say, "it ain't necessarily so," and this may be a reason why the evidence was not overwhelming in the WWC review. *This book will examine the following questions:*

- How do school leaders turn around underperforming schools?
- How does a school leader treat the school's most vulnerable students?
- What are the characteristics of successful school leaders that are social justice centered?
- What problems do these principals face?
- What are the consequences these principals face?

Our research centers on confronting these questions.

Because most of the paradigms of research focus only on results and not on the internal issues of leader beliefs and values (English, 2008), they fail to deal with the essential inner core of leaders who make turning around low-performing schools really work (English & Papa, 2010).

We think it is necessary to talk about these before we deal with the actual practices involved. After all, practices come from values and beliefs about what is and what is not important. And since there is no science of values, one has to speak of these in ways which link actions with beliefs, that is, discerning the congruence between believing and doing.

Here is what we have observed of the beliefs of leaders in turnaround schools. We call this congruence of belief to action a leader's *interiority*.

COMMON INTERIORITY OF
TURNAROUND SCHOOL LEADERS

A Mixture of Self-Efficacy with Optimism

Leaders who take on underperforming or failing schools are skeptics. They are skeptical about most everything except this: *the perfectibility and goodness of humanity.* Nobody goes into school leadership for the money. In many ways school leadership is a kind of "calling," a special sense that the effort required is Herculean but that the rewards, while not monetary, are huge.

If a school leader does not believe that humans are inherently good and understand what it is to be moral, ethical, and kind, there are so many instances where the opposite messages are in abundance that one cannot be sustained in times of trial and trouble which are always there. And we don't mean a kind of naïve optimism, but a hard optimism, a "feet on the ground" optimism centered on the hard realities of life for lots of kids in low-performing or failing schools.

Most of the kids in low-performing or failing schools are not the offspring of the country club set. They are the children of the other sides of the tracks, the trailer parks, low-income housing, one-parent or no-parent families who have early on learned to fend for themselves. They are not the easiest to teach, have counter-stories to the platitudes of the talk shows, and have been exposed to a very dark side of life in America. There is potential there, if you believe it. But you have to believe it. Otherwise you are simply a custodian, a caretaker.

So the successful leader has to be a skeptic. There is no destiny outside of human will. We create our own destinies. While the odds are often stacked against many of the kids and the schools who serve them, nothing is preordained unless we accept it.

Open-Mindedness and Pragmatism

There's no philosopher's stone that turns lead into gold in improving low-performing schools. What works in one context won't necessarily work in another. Part of the reason is that our research methods in examining schools that have been turned around in the past often erase the idiosyncratic elements that were critical in producing them. What we see of leaders who are successful is a commitment to improvement without blind adherence to specific programs, approaches, or elements.

Successful leaders approach their work with a strong belief system regarding the value of public education and the understanding that while all children are different in often fundamental ways, they are similar in many other ways. Successful leaders believe in the innate goodness of humanity and in human potential for growth. They are pragmatic and not dogmatic about putting these beliefs into practice.

Successful leaders learn from their mistakes. They take what didn't work and search for different and better ways to solve the problems they face.

Resiliency and Energy

Successful leaders of turnaround schools are by nature resilient. They know they will be challenged. They know they will suffer some defeats and may even be wounded (Ackerman & Maslin-Ostrowski, 2002).

They understand they will not always prevail in the first instances. They understand they are in a struggle on many different fronts. They have to face internal pessimism about whether all children or "these children" can really succeed at school-defined tasks. They have to face parental indifference or hostility to school authority. They have to confront critics and cynics who have written their schools off or want to turn them over to private companies.

They often have staff that have not been successful elsewhere and have been dumped on their schools because those are the places where fewer teachers want to work. The new Race to the Top guidelines about school firings of principals mean that there will be strong disincentives to even consider working in a low-performing school.

Successful principals of turnaround schools have to have unusual energy. They have to keep their own counsel because there is much bad advice out there and too much pessimism and cynicism about their work.

Competence and Skill Sets

Successful leaders of turnaround schools have developed deep and wide competence and skill sets embodied in the checklists attributed to licensure standards. But the acquisition of those skill sets is no guarantee of success. And too many of those skill sets are embedded in the ideology of neo-liberalism as a value base.

Successful school leaders understand that test scores are important, but they also understand that they are not the be-all and end-all of their efforts to turn around schools (Papa, 2011). They understand that test scores are means to some ends and not necessarily the most important at that. But there is no doubt that successful leaders of turnaround schools are competent educators who know their business. They talk the talk because they have walked the walk.

CONCLUSION

In this book we do not predicate turning around low-performing schools on receiving more resources, though we admit there is plenty of evidence that low-performing schools are too often the oldest buildings in school systems with years of forgotten maintenance, poorly equipped labs, run-down and broken equipment, and classrooms filled with children who are often hungry and poorly clothed. But the human mind has a life of its own and the leadership of such schools does as well.

We do not argue that modern facilities and adequate support staff don't make a difference; we argue that they cannot become excuses for not engaging in turning schools into humane, democratic, and productive places where all children are valued and human potential is nourished and respected. Those are not material things, but spiritual and moral things. Above all else, educational leadership is a spiritual and moral endeavor. Our observation of successful leaders of turnaround schools is vivid testimony to these essential intangibles.

Low-performing or failing schools are similar to high-performing and successful schools in one critical respect: they are human constructions. And as human constructions they are governed by human mores, rules, expectations, and traditions. Imagine being given photographs of two schools that are similar in appearance and told one was high-performing and the other low-performing, then asked to identify which one was which.

One couldn't do it unless something were known about what was going on inside of them. It is the *what was going on inside of them* that we identify in this book. But the major lesson of this effort is that as human constructions we can change schools by changing what goes on inside of them. The key to doing that is *changing what is going on inside the heads of the human beings in them*. That is the challenge of leadership. Leadership is about creating a new mindscape in old landscapes.

While there's no mystery in turning around low-performing or failing schools, there are also no recipes. The essential ingredients can be identified. The key rests in the mind and heart of the leader who has a fundamental understanding of the dynamics of schooling and human motivation and possesses the resiliency and energy to engage in altering the internal landscape of an unsuccessful school. The reasons for the lack of success may be complex and are most certainly interactive.

Unraveling the workings of the school and putting them back together again is a collaborative venture, and is not for the faint of heart. Make no mistake about it. This is hard work. It takes a special kind of educator to do it.

Explicit Leader Beliefs and Actions

We don't believe that leadership is genetic. Leadership is learned. So the leaders of turnaround schools most often are experienced educators. They have acquired a deep understanding of how schools work and the inequities and inequalities they perpetuate in reproducing the larger social order (Barth, 1980; MacLeod, 1987).

Among these are the cultivation of low expectations, reinforced with tracking which results in "an altered 'opportunity structure' detrimental to those in the bottom tracks, because the nature and content of their instruction is systematically different from that of other students" (Joint Center for Political Studies, 1989, p. 17). Successful school leaders have connected how such school routines disadvantage the disadvantaged and send them to the bottom rungs of the socioeconomic system.

Here are the actions we believe are warranted in these conditions. We also believe that a refusal to engage in actions is itself a form of action. We would call that purposeful inaction, to be substituted with purposeful action. But refusing to do harm is the first credo of the physician's code. We believe it is fitting for schools as well.

1. A refusal to accept the status quo as inevitable: We believe our observations and data support the assertion that successful leaders of turnaround schools refuse to accept the status quo. They refuse to engage in actions which perpetuate a culture of low expectations and the inevitability of a permanent underclass based on race and class in America. While they don't deny it exists, they deny it is inevitable and certainly deny it is a sign of a healthy and democratic political system or bodes well for its future.

2. A refusal to accept low-performing or failing schools as permanent features of public education: Successful leaders of turnaround or failing schools do not accept them as permanent features of public education. They see them as social constructs and therefore as changeable. Making them successful means understanding how success is defined and how to relate the workings and complex interactions within such schools to become successful. While they are respectful of humans working in such schools, they are relentless (not ruthless) in working toward consensus of the need for change, connecting actions to that change and working toward higher levels of success. They do not believe that low-performing or failing schools represent having to educate "inferior" students.

3. A commitment to social justice and schools as levers of social change: Successful leaders of turnaround or failing schools envision them as levers of social change, if nothing more than enabling the students to escape the "blame the victim" mental-

ity that is part and parcel of neo-liberalism and the ideology of school choice that in the words of Brian Barry (2007) "hold(s) poor people responsible for choices that arise directly from the relatively limited set of options that poverty (by definition) gives rise to in the market" (p. 87).

Troubleshooting Guide

The troubleshooting guide is designed to deal with specific beliefs, barriers, or problems confronting a leader in a low-performing or failing school.

- No single thing will solve all the problems: Because low-performing or failing schools are complex combinations of interactions and responses, low performance or failure is not the result of any single action or reaction. Rather it is the sum of a series of actions (or lack thereof) and reactions over an extended period of time. Our research shows that schools cannot be turned around on a dime, that lasting change takes many years and may extend over the tenure of more than one leader. No single change, intervention, or innovation will magically turn schools around. Do not search for "quick fixes," as there are none. Look for combinations of things which have to occur simultaneously and sometimes sequentially.
- All constituents must be involved: While the most important group to be involved in school changes are teachers, their input and support will not be enough to carry the day. Parental and student understanding of what is going to be changed and why also are critical features. Develop a comprehensive strategy that involves all the stakeholders in a conversation about change.
- Your commitment must be transparent: The leader's commitment to turning a school around is displayed in every possible situation, and no occasion is too small or unimportant to build commitments and create coalitions to transform the school.

REFERENCES

Ackerman, R., & Maslin-Ostrowski, P. (2002). *The wounded leader: How real leadership emerges in times of crisis.* San Francisco: Jossey-Bass.

Anderson, G. (2010, November). Personal communication.

Anyon, J. (2005). *Radical possibilities, public policy, urban education and a new social movement.* New York: Routledge.

Apple, M. (2006). *Educating the "right" way: Markets, standards, God, and inequality.* New York: Routledge.

Barry, B. (2007). *Why social justice matters.* Cambridge, UK: Polity Press.

Barth, R. S. (1980). *Run school run.* Cambridge, MA: Harvard University Press.

Bloomberg, M., & Klein, J. (March 29, 2010). Making the grade. *Time,* p. 49.

Bolton, C., & English, F. (2009). My head and my heart: De-constructing the historical/hysterical binary that conceals and reveals emotion in educational leadership. In E. Samier and M. Schmidt (eds.), *Emotional dimensions of educational administration and leadership* (pp. 125–142). London: Routledge.

Bolton, C., & English, F. (2010a). Exploring the dynamics of work-place trust, personal agency, and administrative heuristics. In E. Samier & M. Schmidt (eds.), *Trust and betrayal in educational administration and leadership* (pp. 29–42). London: Routledge.

Bolton, C., & English, F. (2010b). De-constructing the logic/emotion binary in educational leadership preparation and practice. *Journal of Educational Administration,* 48 (5), 561–578.

Davis, S. (2004, November). The myth of the rational decision maker: A framework for applying and enhancing heuristic and intuitive decision making by school leaders. *Journal of School Leadership,* 14 (6), 621–652.

Ekman, R. (2010, September 24). The imminent crisis in college leadership. *The Chronicle of Higher Education,* 57 (5), A88.

Emery, K., & Ohanian, S. (2004). *Why is corporate America bashing our public schools?* Portsmouth, NH: Heinemann.

English, F. (1994). *Theory in educational administration.* New York: Harper Collins.

English, F. (2002). Cutting the Gordian knot of educational administration: The theory-practice gap. *UCEA Review,* 44 (1), 1–2.

English, F. (2008). *Anatomy of professional practice: Promising research perspectives on educational leadership.* Lanham, MD: Rowman and Littlefield Education.

English, F. (2010). *Deciding what to teach and test: Developing, aligning, and leading the curriculum, 3rd* ed. Thousand Oaks, CA: Corwin Press.

English, F., & Bolton, C. (2008, January). An exploration of administrative heuristics in the United States and the United Kingdom. *Journal of School Leadership,* 18 (1), pp. 96–119.

English, F. & Papa, R. (2010). *Restoring human agency to educational administration: Status and strategies.* Thousand Oaks, CA: Sage Publications.

Fox, J. (2009). *The myth of the rational market: A history of risk, reward, and delusion on Wall Street.* New York: HarperCollins.

Giroux, H. (2004). *The terror of neoliberalism: Authoritarianism and the eclipse of democracy.* Boulder, CO: Paradigm Publishers.

Harvey, D. (2009). *A brief history of neoliberalism.* Oxford, UK: Oxford University Press.

Gunter, H. (2002). *Leaders and leadership in education.* London: Paul Chapman Publishing.

Institute of Education Sciences-IES. (2008). IES practice guide: Turning around chronically low-performing schools. *What Works Clearinghouse, NCEE 2008-4020.* Retrieved June 2, 2010, from http://ies.ed.gov/ncee/wwc/publications/practiceguides.

Joint Center for Political Studies. (1989). *Visions of a better way: A black appraisal of public schooling.* Washington, DC: Joint Center for Political Studies Press.

MacLeod, J. (1987). *Ain't no makin' it: Leveled aspirations in a low-income neighborhood.* Boulder, CO: Westview Press.

Marshall, C., & Oliva, M. (2006). Building the capacities of social justice leaders. In C. Marshall and M. Oliva (eds.), *Leadership for social justice: Making revolutions in Education* (pp. 1–15). Boston: Pearson.

Marshall, C., & Parker, L. (2006). Learning from leaders' social justice dilemmas. In C. Marshall and M. Oliva (eds.), *Leadership for social justice: Making revolutions in education* (pp. 194–212). Boston: Pearson.

Merriam-Webster. (2010, December). Heuristic, noun. *Merriam-Webster, an Encyclopedia Britannica Company,* 1. Retrieved December 18, 2010, from http://www.merriam-webster.com/dictionary/heuristic.

Nestor-Baker, N.S., & Hoy, W. K. (2001, February). Tacit knowledge of school superintendents: Its nature, meaning, and content. *Educational Administration Quarterly,* 37 (1), 86–129.

Papa, R. (2010). *Personal communication.*

Papa, R. (2011). Standards for educational leaders: Promises, paradoxes and pitfalls. In F. English (ed.), *Second Sage Handbook of Educational Leadership and Administration*. Thousand Oaks, CA: Sage Publications.

Papa, R., Kain, D., & Brown, R. (in press). Who moved my theory? A kitsch exploration of kitsch leadership texts. In B. Irby, G. Brown & R. Lara-Alecio (eds.), *Handbook of Educational Theories*. Charlotte, NC: Information Age Publishing.

Papa [aka Papa-Lewis], R., & Fortune, R. (2002). *Leadership on purpose: Promising practices for African American and Hispanic students*. Thousand Oaks, CA: Corwin.

Ravitch, D. (2010). *The death and life of the great American school system: How testing and choice are undermining education*. New York: Basic Books.

Samier, E. (2005). Toward public administration as a humanities discipline: A humanistic manifesto. *Halduskultuur: Administrative Culture*, 6, 6–59.

Thomas B. Fordham Institute and Broad Foundation. (2003). *Better leaders for America's schools: A manifesto*. Retrieved from http://www.edexcellence.net/doc/Manifesto.pdf.

Thomson, P. (2008, August). Headteacher critique and resistance: A challenge for policy, and for leadership/management scholars. *Journal of Educational Administration and History*, 40 (2), pp. 85–100.

Wiens, J. (2006). Educational leadership as civic humanism. In P. Kellher and R. L. Van Der Bogert (eds.), *Voices for democracy: Struggles and celebrations of transforming leaders* (pp. 199–225). Malden, MA: Blackwell.

2

SELECTING CHANGE MODELS: CHANGING WHAT FOR WHAT?

Management alone will not assure success of the mission. Everyone needs to share in understanding it, believing it and being reminded of it daily if they are to participate in accomplishing it. Together they share the responsibility for the educational plan.

—anonymous urban public school principal,
from Papa & Fortune, 2002

This chapter is a review of the extant turnaround models which exist: technical, political, economically based, social justice models including economics, and cultural capital. The common best practices from the multitude of models will be delineated, including those from professional organizations and the federal reform agenda.

Educational reform models are abundant these days, from charter schools run by public schools to others now run by the for-profit companies or EMOs (Educational Management Organization) (Anderson & Pini, 2005). These models from online to traditional brick-and-mortar schools are primarily the dreams of politicians seeking quick, simplistic, and non-research–based approaches that work only for the short term and sound good in TV sound bites.

We should note that there are change models that really don't change anything, let alone reform anything. In too many cases we find alternatives to what exists cloaked over with new terminology but a very close review finds that the same old assumptions anchor the same old practices. Part of this phenomenon is what Blount (2008) has indicated in the field of educational leadership to be a lack of "a well-developed historical consciousness" (p. 18). She argues that this situation is pervasive in our society because:

> Our capitalist economy demands attention to the earnings in the days ahead; we live in a technology-rich environment that pulls our attention to new advances while dampening our relationships with older technologies; our media push for freshly-minted stories, news, and other entertainments—each with relatively short shelf-lives; our work environments pulsate with demands that we keep up, prepare for and lead change; and we continually search for new solutions to emerging problems, all with the expectation that we are continuing the long, steady march toward a greater society. (p. 18)

However, Blount indicates that such a view privileges the future rather than provides a balanced view of the past. And it makes the past appear as "inferior" or, on a continuum of supposed *progress*, at the lower end of the spectrum.

We see this assumption at work in the many cries for the necessity to engage in change or somehow the nation will be left in the dustbin of history, with the educational system in place being berated for failing to produce the workers and scientists required to maintain world economic dominance. Similarly, the captains of Wall Street and industrialists farm out jobs to third world countries not because their educational systems are better than ours, but because their citizens will work for less than American workers (Emery & Ohanian, 2004).

But this kind of "management-speak" is pervasive in the literature regarding change and reform in education, especially from critics in the private sector who assume that the corporate model of governance is superior to all others. Especially injurious to the democratic function of schooling, the governance structure as embedded in democratically elected school boards is criticized for not being efficient along corporate lines (Gerstner, 2008).

When considering changes in schooling or what to "reform" in education we ought to examine closely the position of the advocates. Nobody is neutral in this conversation and everyone has an agenda. So when school reform is being proposed, who will benefit and who will not?

One of the favorite tactics of the neo-liberals is to bypass any of these questions by accusing defenders of their "reforms" as being more interested in adults and adult welfare than in the children (Hernandez, 2010). So when the neo-liberals advocate merit pay for teachers based on student standardized test scores, those who object are tarred with the brush of indifference to the plight of inner-city children who are "stuck" with poor teachers.

Thus, teacher unions concerned with due process considerations and the shortcomings of test results to determine who is a "good" teacher are slammed with the accusations of protecting incompetence at the expense of what is good for children. The agenda of the neo-liberals in this tactic escapes examination and exposure.

Neo-liberals appear in this scenario disinterested and objective instead of being the mavens of corporatization of the public sphere and advancing a political and economic agenda that is antithetical to the public interest.

Bourdieu & Passeron (1977) would call this a classic case of *misrecognition*, which refers to "the process whereby power relations are perceived not for what they objectively are but in a form which renders them legitimate in the eyes of the beholder" (p. xiii). The strategy of the neo-liberals is to pass off self-interest as disinterest, to present a subjective and partisan agenda as objective and therefore above serious questioning because it is simply *common sense*.

SARASON AND THARP INTERPRETATIONS OF CHANGE

Sarason's four categories of change were: (1) *change theory*; (2) *teaching theory*; (3) *the teaching profession*; and (4) *school power and politics*. Sarason (1990) indicated that the intractability of the school to resist change meant that teachers had to be a major focus for professional development and if teachers did not lead reform efforts it would not succeed. A brief discussion of Sarason's criteria for effective school reform is presented with the interpretation utilized by Tharp.

Change Theory

Based on Sarason's work, Tharp's first category to examine school reforms was collectively called *change theory*. By this he meant that change or reform had to seriously examine the unquestioned bedrock assumptions of schooling, among them what was called by Sarason (1990) the idea of the "encapsulated classroom and school" (p. 111). By this Sarason meant that education occurred best when students were passive, seated in rows, and teachers engaged primarily in whole-class instruction.

A very prescient warning by Sarason has largely gone unheeded in that reformers did not study why previous reforms really failed. Sarason (1990) admonished such would-be "change-agents" when he said, "You apply the conclusions, you deliver the knowledge, you perform the operation as if the object of it is a passive, anesthetized patient" (p. 64).

In medical practice, Groopman (2010) calls this problem an example of a "focusing illusion" which occurs when, basing our predictions on a single change in the status quo, we mistakenly forecast dramatic effects on an overall condition. He similarly warns that in medicine "past efforts to standardize and broadly mandate *best practices* were scientifically misconceived" (p. 13).

This happens when a set of practices are believed to be independent of the patient's response. This resonates with teachers: we know that if students are not listening when we are speaking, then we are not teaching. So, in schools, as in medicine, in many cases so-called "best practices" are *interactive* and *interdependent* with those practices.

Teaching Theory

Tharp's (2008) second category, also based on Sarason's precepts, indicates that a new teaching theory must replace the old (pp. 64–67). By this he meant that the idea that the student is an empty vessel to be filled up by the teacher is outdated and should be scrapped. The student-teacher relationship is one of openness and mutual respect. "Personalized learning," which Sarason explains is "social-personal-transactional in nature," focuses on student-centered learning.

The factory line model of schooling is similarly junked. Parents are enlisted in support of their children and the self-fulfilling prophecy that one cannot expect much from those of low ability or lower class is rejected as inappropriate and reinforcing of negative stereotypes.

The Teaching Profession

Tharp's (2008) third category pertains to the teaching profession (pp. 67–69). In this area Tharp discusses how a significant reform plan must include a view of teachers and teachers' work as one based on their professionalism.

A true reform plan includes teachers as partners and not paid help. Such a plan creates partnerships between schools of education and school systems and rejects the notion that they were only half-trained or half-prepared when they began their teaching careers.

School Power and Politics

As Tharp (2008) notes, this element focuses on "macro-educational issues, namely power issues related to government and the school bureaucracy" (p. 69). Sarason was particularly trenchant in his criticism of top-down reform advanced by government. He wrote,

"One can change curricula, standards, and a lot of other things by legislation or fiat, but if the regularities of the classroom remain un-examined and unchanged, the failure of the reforms is guaranteed" (Sarason, 1990, p. 88).

Before we present Tharp's analysis of these reform plans we want to describe the six reforms he subjected to Sarason's criteria.

THARP'S RESEARCH ON EDUCATIONAL REFORM

John Tharp (2008) studied failed school reforms in the United States. From a list of forty-three reforms tried throughout the nine-teenth and twentieth centuries he selected six that were proffered in their time as having great promise to reform schools. They were the: (1) Lancastrian plan; (2) Age-graded plan; (3) Gary plan; (4) Trump plan; (5) CES plan; and (6) Comer plan. Tharp subjected each of these plans to a qualitative analysis using a rubric of twenty-six in-dicators allocated into four categories derived from the writings of Seymour Sarason (1990; 1993; 1998; 2002; 2004).

The Lancastrian Plan

The Lancastrian plan was named after its originator, Joseph Lan-caster of England. Its attractiveness was that compared to more tra-ditional models of schooling it was cheap and proffered inexpensive education for the poor. For example, Cubberley (1948) noted that after 1817 when the Lancastrian system was introduced in the Phila-delphia schools, the cost per pupil was reduced from twelve dollars per pupil per year to three dollars (p. 663).

The genesis of the idea was that one teacher could take up to a thousand students in one room with the support of helpers called *monitors*. The teacher would give one lesson. This was followed by breaking up the students into smaller recitation rooms under the su-pervision of a monitor who was sometimes simply an older student. Each student would then stand and recite the lesson. When all was done it was repeated.

This model of schooling was supported by Thomas Jefferson, who was a proponent of mass education. It was introduced into the New York City Schools in 1806 and later in at least five other states, Mexico, and Latin America. The deficiencies of the Lancastrian plan were never more evident than after a review by an external committee of its operations in Lancaster, Pennsylvania. The external reviewers wrote:

> On the score of economy and where the main object is to educate a large number of children at the least possible expense, the committee does not doubt that the Lancastrian system has the advantage over every other.
>
> But where thorough and complete instruction is sought for, they are constrained to think that other and more successful methods may be found. And, believing as they do, that the board will consider quality rather than the cheapness of the schools they are about to establish, the committee does not hesitate to recommend the abandonment of a system which they are constrained to believe incurably defective and superficial. (Riddle, 1905, p. 82)

The Lancastrian school was soon to be replaced by another educational reform, the age-graded school, sometimes referred to as the Quincy Graded School Plan, in 1848 (Tyack, 1974, p. 45).

Age-Graded Plan

The Quincy Graded School was an adaptation of the Lancastrian School. Whereas in the latter, children were instructed in a large room and then funneled off to side rooms for recitation, in the former the reform of the Lancastrian model was to abandon the large lecture hall for most of the day and have instruction go on primarily in the recitation rooms (the equivalent of today's self-contained classroom).

Even in those days it was common for students to be grouped by chronological age since the concept of the I.Q. or mental age of students was not invented until 1910, by Alfred Binet in France. On the Quincy Graded School Otto (1954) observed, "It was probably the first grammar school which contained a separate desk and chair for each pupil" (p. 13).

The Quincy Graded School plan proffered three factors that made it supremely attractive to educational reformers of the day. They were:

1. The capability to increase the number of pupils who could recite together within a specific subject;
2. The ability to ease control and planning problems by having all pupils follow the same course of study simultaneously (whole class instruction by today's nomenclature);
3. The allowance of more pupils into each school, which permitted the hiring of more teachers in a uniform manner, thereby encouraging the division of labor within teaching (Cowen, 1967, p. 27).

The quest for control of students and system factors dealing with materiality and money was a prime factor in making the graded school plan attractive to school boards, citizens, and the business community. Today we see the same appeal to hiring non-educators as school leaders advanced by the business community for the same reasons (Eisinger & Hula, 2008). The age-graded school, which is still dominant in American education over one hundred fifty years later, "was primarily advanced to promote managerial control and efficiency rather than for pedagogical enhancements. However, the reforms of the time equated control with instructional effectiveness" (Spring, 1986, pp. 132–140).

The Gary Plan

The Gary Plan was so named because it was first implemented in Gary, Indiana, a community constructed from the ground up next to the new U.S. Steel Corporation's state-of-the-art plant. The school board hired William Wirt as superintendent and he engineered the "platoon school," the moniker of the Gary Plan.

Wirt was a student of John Dewey's and he was opposed to the academic formalism of the traditional school. He combined the idea of *work-study-play* as an antidote and so installed shops, laboratories, gyms, swimming pools, and music rooms, and then divided all students into groups called *platoons*. When one platoon was using the special facilities, another was in classrooms, and another on the playground. While groups of students rotated in these facilities throughout the day, the entire school plant was in full use. The school even ran all year long and in the evenings was used for an adult school.

The Gary Plan was a kind of combination of Dewey's philosophy, scientific management, and the pursuit of efficiency. By 1929, "a nation-wide survey found 1,068 schools in 202 cities throughout the country using the 'platoon' system" (Starr, 1958, p. 728). Yet the Gary Plan was not without its critics.

When Wirt was hired by the mayor of New York City, John Mitchel, to implement the Gary Plan there in 1917, it is estimated that perhaps ten thousand Jewish parents and children rioted over it. They broke windows, interrupted classrooms, and fought with police. One mother railed against the platoon model, saying, "We want our kinder to learn mit der book, der paper, and der pensil and not mit der sewing and der shop" (Tyack, 1974, p. 250).

Eventually, the platoon approach appealed to reformers only as a way to save money, since a 1918 Rockefeller Foundation evaluation found very little to recommend it educationally (Elwell, 1976).

The Trump Plan

J. Lloyd Trump was a professor of education at the University of Illinois. He addressed the question of how to improve schools with a national teacher shortage and how to provide more individualized instruction for students, especially in high school. To deal with the problem, Trump had to confront the iron cage of the school schedule. His idea was to have instruction take place individually and in small and large groups. To make this happen, the flexible schedule had to be developed. This was made possible with the advent of computer technology (Bush & Allen, 1964).

Trump worked with the National Association of Secondary School Principals (NASSP) and was director of its Commission on the Experimental Study of the Utilization of the Staff in the Secondary School (Trump, 1959). The demise of the Trump plan was due to educational leaders' inability to successfully introduce different forms of teaching.

Even in small groups too many teachers continued to lecture as though they were still dealing with whole class instruction (the encapsulated classroom). Also, the independent study aspects of the plan required students to exercise responsibility in governing their time.

For many high schools, independent study became the Achilles heel for the Trump plan (Hackman, 2004, pp. 75–76). Keefe (2004a) noted that "traditional scheduling has locked most of today's schools into self-contained classes . . . [and] LG/SG/IS (large group, small group, independent study) is gone" (p. 169).

The CES (Coalition of Essential Schools) Plan

The CES (Coalition of Essential Schools) was established by Theodore Sizer of Brown University in1984. By 2002 the Coalition consisted of eight hundred schools and twelve centers. The CES plan did not develop a rigid model that every school had to adopt. It did, however, have four basic tenets, which were:

1. All students should be required to engage in serious intellectual work;
2. Classes must be small so students can be well known by their teachers;
3. Teachers must enjoy substantive control over their own work, have time to work collaboratively, and must take co-operative activities for shared groups of students;
4. The family and community must be involved in the school and in their students' work (Keefe, 2004b, p. 7).

In contrast to much of the neo-liberal attack on teachers and schools, "Sizer's approach did not include criticizing teachers or their unions" (Muncey & McQuillan, 1996, pp. 6–7). As one can see almost immediately, one would expect to see very wide levels of variance with schools in the CES.

The Comer Plan

James Comer was a professor at Yale and established an approach to school reform that centered on strong connections between the school, parents, and community while working at the Yale Child Study Center in 1968. The watchwords of Comer's model were "consensus, collaboration and no-fault" (Malloy, 2006, p. 172). Comer's reforms were squarely locked into child development theory (Comer, 1993; 1996; 1997).

Comer's plan included a strong emphasis on site-based management, i.e., "freeing" the schools from the bureaucratic rules of school systems, and the concept of "no-fault" meant that teachers did not blame parents for what their children did not know or could not do.

Comer's approach was based on establishing mutual respect between teachers, parents, and the larger community. And despite some criticisms, Comer schools were very much data-centered on figuring out what worked and what didn't. However, Comer (1996) eschewed evaluating his schools on test scores, saying, "Measuring program outcomes, such as improved student performance on standardized tests is meaningless unless there is a commensurate assessment of the level and quality of program implementation" (p. 123).

WHY THESE REFORM PLANS FAILED

Using Sarason's (1990) criteria, Tharp's research delved into the details as to why these six well-publicized school reform efforts all failed to deliver the expected changes. His data are summarized in Table 2.1 and show that none of the reform plans were effective on all of Sarason's criteria. Therefore they eventually failed, even

Table 2.1. A Summary of Tharp's Six Failed School Plans on Sarason's *Predictable Failure* Criteria

Tharp's Plans	Change Theory	Teaching Theory	Teaching Profession	School Power & Politics
1. Lancastrian Plan	Sometimes effective	Not effective	Not effective	Sometimes effective
2. Age-Graded Plan	Sometimes effective	Not effective	Not effective	Sometimes effective
3. Gary Plan	Sometimes effective	Sometimes effective	Not effective	Sometimes effective
4. Trump Plan	Sometimes effective	Sometimes effective	Sometimes effective	Sometimes effective
5. CES Plan	Sometimes effective	Very effective	Sometimes effective	Sometimes effective
6. Comer Plan	Effective	Very effective	Sometimes effective	Sometimes effective

though the Coalition of Effective Schools plan and the Comer Plan were rated "sometimes effective" to "very effective" on all of Sarason's criteria. If Sarason (1990) was correct, for a reform to be successful it would have to be rated "effective to very effective" on all of the criteria and be sustainable at those levels over time.

This requirement is a very tall order indeed because it involves all parties working with and impacted by schools and the relationships among and between them. Those relationships are rarely static or even stable over an extended period of time. We now examine this phenomenon of reform.

WHO BENEFITS FROM SCHOOL REFORM?

Reforming schools is neither a neutral activity nor a project of objectivity. The interests of the parties who are advocates of educational reform must include an examination of their agendas for change.

What constitutes a "reform" depends upon who is proposing it. For example, if a person proposing change is a neo-liberal, then that individual's "reform" may mean introducing forms of competition for educational resources that would have gone to the public schools alone. If, on the other hand, a second person sees the purpose of schools is to change the existing social structure so that it is fairer and more equitable, then the neo-liberal "reform" is anathema because it will solidify the socioeconomic status quo. The bottom line is that *a reform is not a reform is not a reform.*

Kowalski and Brunner (2005) have identified a continuum of reform which indicates that on one end are those who want the schools to deal with "poverty, abuse, and dysfunctional homes; they favor increased fiscal resources, even if more funding results in a further erosion of local control" (p. 158). On the other end are those "who view schools as being inefficient and insufficiently attentive to academic standards; they favor creating competition through concepts such as vouchers, tax credits, and charter schools" (p. 158).

Figure 2.1 shows the Kowalski-Brunner continua along with a designation of answering the question of reform sponsorship by

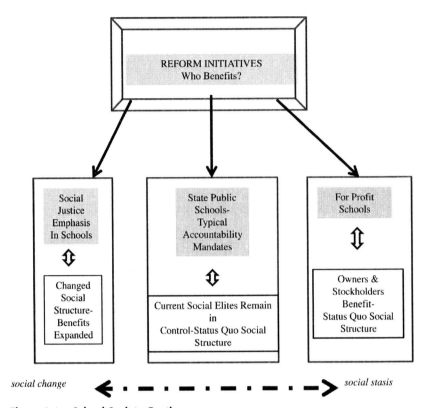

Figure 2.1. School-Society Continuum

asking the question: *who benefits* from the reform if it is implemented? A sociological perspective offered by Blau and Scott (1962) proposed that organizations such as schools could be differentiated from others by looking deeply at the issue of *cui bono*, i.e., who really benefits from these organizations.

From their work we can envision two levels of beneficiaries, the primary beneficiary and a secondary beneficiary. For example, teacher unions are classified as *mutual benefit associations* along with religious groups, guilds, and political parties because the primary beneficiaries of their activities are the members. In the case of teacher unions, secondary beneficiaries may well be students or the larger society.

This may also be the case with political parties. In the case of forprofit businesses or agencies, the primary beneficiaries are the owners and/or stockholders. If a business renders some sort of service, the receivers of that service may be a secondary beneficiary. But in the world of for-profit work, if a business doesn't make money it ceases to exist.

Figure 2.1 illustrates these differences. To the far left are those who advocate reforms which will change the socioeconomic-political structure of our society. These may be advocates for social justice. They see schools as the means to alter social consciousness and practice. In the middle are those who push a variety of account-ability schemes such as more standardized testing and curriculum standards. Their proposals would leave the larger social structure intact. In the far right column are the neo-liberal organizations and right-wing think tanks that push for more competition for public resources for the public schools. Their proposals, sponsored by a hefty chunk of the business elites (Emery & Ohanian, 2004), would solidify the social status quo and reinforce the position of advantage they already enjoy.

Figure 2.1 also shows that for social justice issues to be ad-dressed the school cannot remain a conservative force to retain the socioeconomic-political advantages enjoyed by some, but not all, of the population. The school-societal nexus remains the flashpoint for social reform and the tackling of the larger societal inequities and inequalities. True school reform is not for the faint of heart nor the transient politician or tinkerer.

The typical governmental or business-backed accountability change agenda is an embodiment of many facets of warmed-over scientific management. Much, if not all, of the national movement toward leadership standards includes a "one size fits all" mantra (Papa, 2011) which amounts to the erasure of the context for leader-ship which is the fulcrum of being successful as a leader.

Not only that, but mandated accountability models assume that, when recommending change, the schools or school systems with which and upon which the formulae are recommended are largely inert entities. So if a generic list of attributes or skills is "the" model for successful site turnaround efforts, then the school is static in-stead of what we have learned in our research, which is that schools are never static and much of the change agenda in turning them around is *reactive* and *interactive* with actions school leaders may take.

THE OBAMA/DUNCAN REFORM AGENDA

The election of Barack Obama to the U.S. presidency potentially promised re-examining historic obstacles to the education of minorities and the poor in U.S. public schools. Unfortunately, as observed by Chennault (2010), "President Obama's education agenda is, broadly speaking, indistinguishable from that of his predecessor" (p. 31).

The Obama/Duncan *Blueprint for Reform* (U.S. Department of Education, 2010, March) supports that all students must be included in a rigorous and fair accountability system and that all students must be supported in their diversity of learning. To quote:

> This blueprint builds on the significant reforms already made in response to the American Recovery and Reinvestment Act of 2009 around four areas: (1) Improving teacher and principal effectiveness to ensure that every classroom has a great teacher and every school has a great leader; (2) Providing information to families to help them evaluate and improve their children's schools, and to educators to help them improve their students' learning; (3) Implementing college- and career-ready standards and developing improved assessments aligned with those standards; and (4) Improving student learning and achievement in America's lowest-performing schools by providing intensive support and effective interventions. (p. 3)

The Obama/Duncan blueprint is a federal mandate to the states that may or may not come with the funding required. It is essentially a one-size-fits all approach and has received criticism for its lack of research support to its pronouncements. According to Mathis and Welner (2010), " . . .there is a general neglect of peer-reviewed research and an over-reliance on information gathering from special interest groups, think tanks, government documents and media reports" (p. 5).

The Obama/Duncan approach does not mandate any internal changes, nor does it deal with issues of change policy or pedagogical changes. The *required* four models school districts must use to turn around the lowest-performing schools in each state are described in the Blueprint for Reform. All would fail Sarason's criteria. They are the:

- *Transformation model*: Replace the principal, strengthen staffing, implement a research-based instructional program, provide extended learning time, and implement new governance and flexibility.
- *Turnaround model*: Replace the principal and rehire no more than 50 percent of the school staff, implement a research-based instructional program, provide extended learning time, and implement new governance structure.
- *Restart model*: Convert or close and reopen the school under the management of an effective charter operator, charter management organization, or education management organization.
- *School closure model*: Close the school and enroll students who attended it in other, higher-performing schools in the district (U.S. Department of Education, 2010, March, p. 12).

Five percent of all schools must, under the directives of the blueprint, be identified as Challenge states, districts, and schools. These lowest-performing schools will be assessed on student achievement, growth, and matriculation numbers. Once a school, district, and/or state is identified, one of the four turnaround models *is required to ensue*.

Ongoing growth for Challenge schools, districts, and states will be assessed by data-driven interventions, expanding learning time, providing supplemental services, offering greater public school choice, and so on. And, finally, if growth is not able to be measured quickly enough, the cutting of ESEA funds to the schools, districts, or state will happen.

According to Ravitch and Mathis (2010), there is little research to support the four turnaround models. And the severe sanctions that face Challenge schools and districts that fail could disproportionally affect those students who are most needy: English language learners and high-poverty communities.

Some models of change endorse top-down approaches. Per Senge, Kleiner, Roberts, Ross, Roth, and Smith (1999): "Significant change only occurs when it is driven from the top" (p. 10). Clearly, the federal imposition on public schools believes this change model approach: the Blueprint for Reform is meant to "rescue the rest of us from recalcitrant, noncompetitive institutions" (Senge et al. p. 11).

However, Tharp's research using Sarason's criteria indicates that while change can be initiated from the top, it can rarely be sustained from the top. Unless reform is seen by all parties as advantageous to them it will ultimately fail.

HEURISTICS FOR THE ACTIVIST LEADER

Heuristic 5: Educational reform is complex, multifaceted, and interactive. There have been many attempts at educational reform in the U.S. over a two-hundred-year period. While some were initially successful, none have been able to be sustained except the graded school, which is one of the few exceptions to sustainability. However, the graded school carries enormous educational baggage and continues to be a major barrier to breaking what Sarason (1990) has called "the encapsulated classroom" (p. 111) tradition.

Educational reform cannot be considered an approach involving a simple checklist which is enacted upon stable organizational entities. Schools are dynamic and fluid despite how they may appear to outsiders. Any reform that attempts to change internal dynamics must be considered interactional and not static. Schools are living organisms and changes that are "successful" in one context may not be so in another because the internal dynamics and relationships vary from site to site.

Heuristic 6: The motivations and goals of educational reformers are not the same. Any study of the history of the reformers of education in the U.S. will show that some were prompted by altruistic goals of educating the masses while others were looking for cheap and quick educational fixes. Many reformers are still looking for quick fixes and too many believe that the corporate model of "one size fits all" and top-down change will reform the schools so that they work for everyone and not simply the well-to-do. In this they are mistaken.

Reformers do not all agree on what constitutes a reform. Many reforms are profoundly anti-democratic. While the rhetoric about changing schools is usually about students and learning, many reforms have little or anything to do with learning. Rather they are about imposing a "for-profit" mind-set on the schools where the major beneficiaries are not students at all, but the owners and stockholders.

Heuristic 7: Many reforms have little to do with social justice. Many educational reforms propose changes that have little to do with altering the socioeconomic-political status quo. Schools continue to act as conservative social agents that reproduce the culture and status of those in control of the country and its economic agents. Some reforms benefit those who are now in control of the schools and enhance their position. Not everyone benefits from reforming schools. It all depends on who is defining the reform and what is the content of it.

CONCLUSION

School reform is not a neutral endeavor. Not all reformers want the same things. Not all reforms question bedrock assumptions. There are those who simply want schools to cost less. They are interested in efficiency. There are those who want schools to educate pupils better, but only some pupils. They are the elitists. There are those who want schools to confront the growing economic divide between the haves and have-nots of our society. They want schools to do different things than they do now, teach in different ways, and become more broad-based with all segments of the population.

No matter how the reform agenda is defined, schools cannot be considered inert entities which are the same everywhere. What works in some places will not always work in other places. Schools are interactive and reactive with any number of interventions. The key to successful reform lies in the preparation of school leaders who understand that context is the major determinant of what works and what doesn't.

Explicit Leader Beliefs and Actions

As we stated in chapter 1 the leaders of turnaround schools most often are experienced educators. Successful school leaders have connected how such school routines disadvantage the disadvantaged and send them to the bottom rungs of the socioeconomic system.

In this chapter we presented two change models and the criteria that define very effective change processes. So, here are the actions we believe are warranted in these conditions.

1. A commitment to a participatory process: We believe our observations and data support the assertion that successful leaders of turnaround schools lead by inclusive styles. The participation of all "players" in the design and execution of the change processes is critical for the success of the reform.
2. A commitment to understanding who is doing the speaking: Successful leaders of turnaround or failing schools do not accept such labels as permanent features of public education that serve as poorly disguised benchmarks. Knowing where the reform agenda is philosophically based pushes the school leader to ensuring that labels serve little purpose in the process of "very effective" school processes.
3. A commitment to social justice: As we have said, school reform is not for the faint of heart. The school-societal nexus remains the flashpoint for social reform and the tackling of the larger societal inequities and inequalities.

Troubleshooting Guide

- Concentrate on context: Beware of checklists which indicate explicitly or implicitly that if the items on the list are all marked off, reform success will always be the result. Context is the key to successful reform. It is rarely 100 percent the same and the actors and interactions are almost always different. So understand what is different about your context from others. What are the unique facets of your students, teachers, parents and your community? How do they interact and come together?

- Address teaching and learning issues to close educational gaps. Sarason's (1990; 1993; 1998; 2002; 2004) work shows that without addressing the traditional ideas of teaching and learning in schools, not much will change much in them. Schools will continue to perpetuate the socioeconomic status quo. Reformers who want only to impose a new model of governance will only, perhaps, resolve governance issues, whatever they may be. Ask what kinds or reform will reform what? Sarason (2004) said it best: "Teaching is not a science; it is an art fusing ideas, obligations, the personal and interpersonal. The chemistry of that fusion determines whether or how subject matter matters to the students" (p. 199).

REFERENCES

Anderson, G., & Pini, M. (2005). Educational leadership and the new economy: Keeping the "public" in public schools. In F. English (ed.), *The Sage handbook of educational leadership: Advances in theory, research, and practice* (pp. 216–236). Thousand Oaks, CA: Sage.

Blau, P., & Scott, W. (1962). *Formal organizations.* San Francisco: Chandler Publishing Company.

Blount, J. (2008). History as a way of understanding and motivating: Social justice work in education. In T. Townsend and I. Bogotch (eds.), *Radicalizing educational leadership: Dimensions of social justice* (pp. 17–38). Rotterdam: Sense Publishers.

Bourdieu, P., & Passeron, J. C. (1977). *Reproduction in education, society and culture*. London: Sage.

Bush, R., & Allen, D. (1964). *A new design for high school education*. New York: Harcourt, Brace & World.

Chennault, R. (2010, May 19). Obama-era education policy. *Education Week, 29*, 30–31.

Comer, J. (1993). *Making a difference for children*. New York: Teachers College, Columbia University.

Comer, J. (1996). *Rallying the whole village: The Comer process for reforming education*. New York: Teachers College Press, Columbia University.

Comer, J. (1997). *Waiting for a miracle: Why schools can't solve our problems—and how we can*. New York: Penguin Books.

Cowen, P. (1967). How the graded school system developed. In M. Franklin (ed.), *School organization: Theory and practice*. Chicago: Rand McNally & Company.

Cubberley, E. (1948). *The history of education*. Boston: Houghton-Mifflin.

Eisinger, P., & Hula, R. (2008). Gunslinger school administrators: Nontraditional leadership in urban school systems in the United States. In J. Munro (ed.), *Educational leadership* (pp. 111–126). Boston: McGraw-Hill.

Elwell, R. (1976, July). The Gary plan revisited. *American Education, 12* (6), 16–22.

Emery, K., & Ohanian, S. (2004). *Why is corporate America bashing our public schools?* Portsmouth, NH: Heinemann.

Gerstner, L. (2008, December 1). Lessons from 40 years of education "reform." *The Wall Street Journal*, p. A23.

Groopman, J. (2010, February 11). Health care: Who knows "best"? *New York Review of Books, 43* (2), 12–15.

Hackman, D. (2004). Flexible scheduling to promote personalized learning. In J. Frymier & R. Joekel (eds.), *Changing the school learning environment: Where we do stand after decades of reform?* (pp. 73–94). Lanham, MD: Scarecrow Education.

Hernandez, J. (2010, December 26). "We weren't bold enough," New York City departing schools chief says. *New York Times*, p. 32.

Keefe, J. (2004a). School structure. In J. Frymier and R. Joekel (eds.), *Changing the school learning environment: Where do we stand after decades of reform?* Lanham, MD: Scarecrow Education.

Keefe, J. (2004b). Comprehensive school renewal; MSP, LEC, and CES. In J. Frymier and R. Joekel (eds.), *Changing the school learning environment:*

Where do we stand after decades or reform? (pp. 7–26). Lanham, MD: Scarecrow Education.

Kowalski, T., & Brunner, C. C. (2005). The school superintendent: Roles, challenges, and issues. In F. English (ed.), *The Sage handbook of educational leadership: Advances in theory, research and practice* (pp. 142–167). Thousand Oaks, CA: Sage.

Malloy, W. (2006). Comer school development plan. In F. English (ed.), *Encyclopedia of educational leadership and administration*, Vol. 2 (pp. 171–173). Thousand Oaks, CA: Sage.

Mathis, W. J., & Welner, K. G. (2010). Assessing the research base for a blueprint for reform. In William J. Mathis and Kevin G. Welner (Eds.), *The Obama education blueprint: Researchers examine the evidence*: A publication of a Volume in the NEPC series: National Education Policy Center. Charlotte, NC: Information Age Publishing, Inc.

Muncey, D., & McQuillan, P. (1996). *Reform and resistance in schools and classrooms.* New Haven, CT: Yale University Press.

Otto, H. (1954). *Elementary school organization and administration.* New York: Appleton-Century Crofts, Inc.

Papa, R. (2011). Standards for educational leaders: Promises, paradoxes and pitfalls. In F. English (ed.), *Second Sage Handbook of Educational Leadership and Administration.* Thousand Oaks, CA: Sage Publications.

Papa [aka Papa-Lewis], R., & Fortune, R. (2002). *Leadership on purpose: Promising practices for African American and Hispanic students.* Thousand Oaks, CA: Corwin.

Ravitch, D., & Mathis, W. J. (2010). A review of college- and career ready students: A U.S. Department of Education research summary in support of its blueprint for reform. In William J. Mathis and Kevin G. Welner (eds.), *The Obama education blueprint: Researchers examine the evidence*: A publication of a Volume in the NEPC series: National Education Policy Center. Charlotte, NC: Information Age Publishing, Inc.

Riddle, W. (1905). *One hundred and fifty years of school history in Lancaster, Pennsylvania.* Lancaster, PA: Published by the author.

Sarason, S. B. (1990). *The predictable failure of educational reform: Can we change course before it's too late?* San Francisco: Jossey-Bass.

Sarason, S. B. (1993). *Letters to a serious education president.* Newbury Park, CA: Corwin Press.

Sarason, S. B. (1998). *Charter schools: Another flawed educational reform?* New York: Teachers College.

Sarason, S. B. (2002). *Educational reform: A self-scrutinizing memoir*. New York: Teachers College Press.

Sarason, S. B. (2004). *And what do you mean by learning?* Portsmouth, NH: Heinemann.

Senge, P., Kleiner, A., Roberts, C., Ross, R., Roth, G., & Smith, B. (1999). *The dance of change: The challenge of sustaining momentum in learning organizations*. New York: Doubleday.

Spring, J. (1986). *The American school 1642–1985*. New York: Longman.

Starr, H. (1958). *Dictionary of American biography, 11, Part 1, Supplement 1*. New York: Charles Scribner's Sons.

Tharp, J. (2008). *Breaking the cycle of failed school reform: What five failed reforms tell us*. Lanham, MD: Rowman & Littlefield Education.

Trump, J. (1959). *Images of the future: A new approach to the secondary school*. Urbana, IL: National Association of Secondary School Principals.

Tyack, D. (1974). *The one best system*. Cambridge, MA: Harvard University Press.

U.S. Department of Education. (2010, March). *A blueprint for reform: The reauthorization of the elementary and secondary education act*. Alexandria, VA: U.S. Department of Education.

3

ACTIVIST LEADERSHIP TO IMPROVE SCHOOLING AND LIFE CHANCES

When schools send correspondence out in only English, hold parent meetings during hours that parents work or if the meetings are held only in English when other languages are prominent in the community, the message says, "Your input is unimportant to the school [as] we don't think that you are important enough for us to communicate with you in a language that you understand."

—anonymous urban public school principal,
from Papa & Fortune, 2002

The popular rhetoric about American public schools, life chances, and the ladder to the good life is that *education is the great equalizer.* Education is the means by which the poor can extract themselves from the bottom socioeconomic rungs of society and climb the ladder to success and material wealth. All that is necessary is to come to school, be diligent, and work hard, and those without the benefit of high birth or wealth can reach the same levels as the more privileged and well-off members of our society.

This stereotypical perspective is today an impossible ideal for many schools and the teachers and administrators who work in them. Consider the letter that appeared in *Education Week in* 2011, written by a fifth-grade teacher in California who works in a barrio.

The teacher indicated he had thirty-two students in his class, of which 50 percent had set foot in a jail or a prison to visit family members recently. Few of his students were on grade level. Eleven of his class were retained and five more were in special education. He recounts that one of his students was shot dead trying to rob a local bank. He pleads, "It's not bad teaching that got things to the current state of affairs. We don't teach in failing schools. We teach in failing communities" (Karrer, 2011, p. 23).

THE CHANGING AND CHALLENGING DEMOGRAPHICS FOR SCHOOLING

Here are some factual statistics which will be impacting public education in America (Vinovskis, 2009, pp. 208–214).

- The percentage of the U.S. population that is foreign-born has risen from 5 percent in 1960 to 12 percent in 2005. Many of the recent immigrants have few employable skills and do not speak English.
- The median income of Hispanic families was less than two-thirds of white families' median income in 2005.
- More than one of every six children in the U.S. today lives in poverty. In 2005, 14.4 percent of white children lived in poverty compared to 34.5 percent for African-American children and 28.3 percent of Hispanic children.
- More than one-fifth of elementary and secondary school students in 2004 had at least one foreign-born parent.
- In 1960 about 9 percent of the children under eighteen lived with a single parent. In 2005 the number living with a single parent increased to 28 percent.

- The number of white children living with a single parent in 2006 was 18 percent. For African-American and Hispanics it was 51 and 25 percent, respectively.

These statistics vividly illustrate the changing nature of American society at the bottom and middle-income levels. A view of the top stratum of American society indicates that "the top 10 percent of Americans now own 70 percent of the country's wealth while the top 5 percent own more than everyone else put together" (Freedland, 2007, as cited in Irvin, 2008, p. 12).

In addition, in comparison to sixteen OECD (Organization for Economic Co-operation and Development, 2001) nations, the U.S. had the highest rate of child poverty and the lowest social expenditure as a percentage of GDP [gross domestic product] (Mishel, Bernstein, & Allegretto, 2007). The comparison countries included Italy, Ireland, Spain, Australia, Canada, United Kingdom, Germany, France, the Netherlands, Austria, Switzerland, Belgium, Norway, Finland, Sweden, and Denmark.

In 2003 the U.S. had the highest infant mortality rate of any country in the OECD. And in another study, America had the highest *persistence of poverty rate* of any reviewed. This means that, once in poverty, a family was more likely to remain there in the U.S. than in many other nations. Irvin (2008) commented that "the persistence of poverty appears to be strongly correlated with the level of inequality that [one] obtains in any given country" (p. 94).

Irvin's observation is reinforced by a study conducted by Hertz (2005) of 6,273 African American and white families' intergenerational economic mobility over thirty-two years and two generations. Hertz (2005) found that black families' rate of upward mobility was considerably lower than that of whites. For example, "while only 17 percent of whites born to the bottom decile of family income remained there as adults, for blacks the figure was 42 percent" (p. 165).

The huge disparity between the rich and the poor in the United States is second in the world, behind only China (*The Economist*,

2011, p. 8). And that inequality is not related to educational achievement at all. Rather, as Hacker and Pierson (2010) have illustrated, it is the direct result of the politics played out in Washington where vested moneyed interests have worked against the children of the poor "as the game has become more tilted against them, their economic standing growing less secure, their chance of climbing the economic ladder stagnating" (p. 290).

Blaming the schools for this economic disparity is a charade, a convenient and vulnerable target where the victims of the policies which expand the wealth of a few are masked in blame and fake reform talk.

ABOUT LIFE CHANCES IN AMERICA

From care within the womb through mother's nutrition to medical care at birth, income and wealth decide equal or unequal treatment. Prenatal care ranges from classes covering pregnancy, availability of books regarding the growing time in the womb, to leaving work for doctor's appointments that does not dock the mother. Medical choices come to those of wealth—whether to use a midwife, give birth at home, and so on.

Once the baby is born, who the parents are begins the environmental differences. Hart and Risley, 1995 (as noted in Barry, 2005, p. 51), state:

> Longitudinal data showed that in every day interactions at home, the average (rounded) number of words children heard per hour was 2,150 in the professional families, 1,250 in the working-class families and 620 in the welfare families . . . both quantity and quality of parents speech correlated very strongly with children's measured linguistic ability at the age of three.

Barry (2005) notes other factors that affect parents' unequal cultural resources. These include: qualifications and pay of those who provide child care; different school environments; how well a child is fed; school attendance problems, etc. Children lose out if their parents cannot afford to take time off to look after them when they are sick or deal with crises. This requires paid leave for parents (p. 54). In a study done in 2000,

> it was found that those children who scored in the bottom quarter on reading and mathematics were significantly more likely to have working parents who lacked paid holidays, sick leave and job flexibility . . . controlling for differences in family income and in parental education, marital status, and total hours parents worked, the more hours parents had to be away from home after school in the evening, the more likely their children were to test in the bottom quartile on achievement tests.
>
> More remarkably still, perhaps, after controlling for differences parents that had to work at night were still 2.7 times as likely to have a child who had been suspended from school . . . those who already have the disadvantage of being poor have it compounded by Dickensian conditions of work. (Barry, 2005, p. 55)

Barry (2005) continues to question why, if we pursue social justice, intensive research efforts have not been devoted to find the best ways to overcome the disadvantages children come to school with "and continue to suffer from—as a consequence of their home and neighborhood environment" (p. 55).

THE HOME AND SCHOOL NEXUS

The perceptions and roles of parents and how we build social capital with them mean we must guide parents in their understanding of the "school game." This is crucial to obtaining parental support in the home environment. Strengthening connections between the home, school, and community is a fundamental part of the successful school practices. The Papa and Fortune (2002) research identified that parents in successful Hispanic and African American high schools were assisted by the schools to help in their child's classroom, as an example.

The first demand of social justice is "to change the environments in which children are born and grow up so as to make them as equal as possible" (Barry, 2005, p. 58). A socially just education system minimizes the effects on children's opportunities from their parents' social and economic position. "School choice is just the final straw, in which the effects of parental advantages and disadvantages are multiplied by placing the enormous premium on know-how and resources" (p. 66).

These, Barry believes, can be overcome through social justice largely determined by the political processes that mobilize in opposition to "moves designed to disturb the process by which the advantages of one generation are transmitted to the next" (p. 69).

How one views cultural differences between the teachers and the parents/community is evidenced by how schools view the role of parents. Often, schools view parents as obstacles to move around with as little engagement as possible, especially if they speak a language other than English. This is not how we empower parents in becoming involved with their child's school. There is a certain amount of arrogance in the attitude of school officials regarding linguistic communication.

Perhaps it is best illustrated by a quotation from Winston Churchill. When Britain was a world power he said, "Everybody has a right to pronounce foreign names as he chooses" (Enright, 2001, p. 76). Only a person who is on top of the power hierarchy can adopt such a cultural stance. And it is a reminder of their power to treat you as they please because they don't have to treat you otherwise. It is not a respectful approach designed to win confidence, trust, or friends.

Delgado-Gaitan (1990) notes the optimal role for home-school communication with Spanish-speaking families. She believes literacy is a socially constructed activity between the school and the home. This posture underscores the importance of mutuality and respect in constructing purposeful communication.

Likewise, schools need to be concerned with student absences all through kindergarten to high school. Habits are formed young. Expectations that are high ensure students come to school. Schools track students to ensure they are correctly funded from state and federal dollars.

Chang (September, 2010) notes five myths teachers and principals have about student attendance: 1) Students don't start missing a lot of school until middle or high school; 2) Absences in the early grades don't really affect academics; 3) Most schools already know how many students are chronically absent; 4) There's not much that schools can do to improve attendance; it's up to the parents; and, 5) The federal government has no role in reducing chronic absence. All myths!

The importance of working with families and students to attend schools is critical to understand as it directly confronts the poverty many families live in. Chronic absences, such as students staying home to care for sick siblings because their parents do not get paid sick days, have no daytime transportation, are homeless, or have religious day observances, require the school to move beyond the surface to deeper issues.

Changing our perspective on school attendance to one that is concerned with all the elements of family life is an example of activist and purposeful leadership.

SCHOOLING AND HARD CHOICES

On the institutional integrity side of public schooling, poor and crumbling school buildings and novice teachers are often found in urban schools. Instead of finding small class sizes and increased funding to work with English language learners who have strong mentor teachers and principals, the opposite is often found.

Activist and purposeful leadership understands the complexity of today's students. Reform efforts that focus on opening up opportunities through school choice for students are founded on assumptions that all students and parents have equal funding to attend schools of their choice, and that they all have the same ability to understand how to make an informed choice. Likewise, public schools may have the best teachers leave for alternative schools that *can self-select their students*.

CHAPTER 3

Perhaps an ongoing testimony to the difficulties faced by the nation's inner-city school systems is the crisis of public education in Detroit, Michigan, called by some the worst-performing school district in the U.S. (Dolan, 2011). Detroit has been losing students to outlying school districts and charter schools. It has a $1.025 billion budget but carries a deficit of $327 million. The most pressing problem is how to assure lenders who meet the system's payroll that the district won't fall into bankruptcy.

The obvious financial solutions have been implemented: closing schools, laying off teachers, privatizing school services, and putting teachers on a form of merit pay. But these solutions don't really address the true nature of the problem at all: the lack of understanding and plight of the issues facing families who live in Detroit.

The privatization of schools avoids the main issue, that is, no one has any responsibility to improve a public service if it has been privatized around choice because the blame can be placed on those who made "poor choices" or who are labeled as lazy, ignorant, or stupid. The installation of choice plans means once again poor schools are blamed on the victims who attend them and their families (Ravitch, 2010).

Perhaps the best example of how victims are blamed for the conditions in which they find themselves is Charles Murray, a scholar at the right-wing think tank the American Enterprise Institute and co-author with R. Herrnstein of the book *The Bell Curve* (1994), widely considered to be racist. This book was an argument, largely based on outdated thinking, that poor performance was caused by the lack of intelligence as measured by I.Q. and that federal programs such as Head Start were a waste of time and money because the children were too stupid to profit from them.

Kincheloe and Steinberg (1997) have studied the so-called research cited by Herrnstein and Murray and noted that a large amount of it was financed by a long-standing white supremacist organization (The Pioneer Fund) that proves "that African-Americans are disproportionately poor because of their genetic inferiority" (p. 38).

Murray (2005) made the same argument in the aftermath of Hurricane Katrina when he vastly oversimplified the condition of thousands of people forced from their homes who were mostly poor African Americans. He consistently refers to them as "these people" and his racism is undisguised:

> These people are rightly the objects of an outpouring of help from around the country, but their troubles are relatively easy to resolve. Tell the man where a job is, and he will take it. Tell the mother where the school is, and she will get her children into it. Other images show us the face of the hard problem: those of the looters and thugs, and those of inert women doing nothing to help themselves or their children. They are the underclass. (p. A18)

African Americans face what Boykin (1986) has called "a triple quandary" in the U.S. First they have two identities, that is, they are like whites in that they are human, but they are simultaneously different, and that difference is how whites define their hegemonic place in respect to them. So, like other groups, African Americans are bicultural. But in the last instance they are how white America defines its "otherness" to itself. The "triple quandary" then makes assimilation much more difficult than other immigrant groups have encountered.

Boykin (1986) indicates that the African American cultural patterning is *noncommensurable* with the Euro-American patterning, which is the mainstream culture reflected in schools. And the Euro-American dominance "defines all other values as essentially illegitimate" (Boykin, 1986, p. 66). The contrast between the Euro-American and African-American cultural positions is shown in table 3.1 below. It has been constructed from descriptions of the two cultures by Boykin (1986, p. 63).

Boykin (1986) indicates that the African-American cultural reality makes the black experience in schools controlled by the Euro-American cultural reality especially problematic. He indicates that the Euro-American "ideology that informs those institutions [schools] is a profound negation of the most central attributes of African culture" (p. 63).

Norton-Smith (2010) has made a similar observation regarding Native American cultural perspectives and the Euro-American view

Table 3.1. A Comparison of Euro-American and African-American Cultural Patterning Differences Based on Boykin (1986)

Orientation Toward	African-American Cultural Tradition	Euro-American Cultural Tradition
Overall cultural orientation	Expressive individualism and communalism; possessions belong to the community at large, uniqueness is valued	Possessive individualism and egalitarian conformity; private property is an inalienable right, sameness is valued
Attitude toward nature	Harmony with nature and spiritualism	Mastery over nature and an emphasis on materialism
Major metaphors	Organic metaphors	Mechanistic metaphors
Bodily orientation	Expressive movement	Compressive orientation toward impulse control
View of other cultures	Emphasizes interconnectedness	Emphasizes separateness
Time orientation	Toward events and oral culture	Clock orientation based on print
Orientation toward other people	Person-to-person emphasis with personal orientation toward objects	Person-to-object emphasis with impersonal (objective) orientation toward people

when he too indicated that the two cultures were "incommensurable" and that the perspective of the world as constructed by Euro-Americans based on "deductive validity and inductive rightness, utility and simplicity—are culturally biased against non-Western world versions" (p. 120).

The presence of such bias is one of the major reasons Maynor (2011) found in her study of Native American students in North Carolina that they dropped out of school in disproportionate numbers and they had the lowest four-year graduation rate of any ethnic group in the state (p. 163). She also cited a report by the North Carolina State Advisory Council on Indian Education in 2003 that concluded that:

American Indian students who dropped out of the state's public schools were not necessarily academically weak students or students who disliked schools and learning. Instead these youth were bright and talented students who excelled in elementary school and lost their way when reaching middle or high school choosing to leave school after consecutive years of feeling disconnected to, ignored by, and unimportant to the adults and the majority student population around them. (Maynor, 2011, pp. 165–66)

The constructed reality of the dominant school culture in the U.S. is neither neutral nor universal. It is one that has been assembled to support the interests of the majoritarian elites. Barry (2005) summarizes this sociopolitical hegemony aptly:

In every society, the prevailing belief system has been largely created by those with the most power—typically, elderly males belonging to the majority ethnic and religious group, who also run the dominant institutions of society. It is notable, for example, that almost all religions rationalize a subordinate position for women and explain that inequalities of fortune are to be accepted as part of God's great (if mysterious) plan. (p. 27)

This role of the school in defining the only legitimate version of reality open to its young is an example of Bourdieu and Passeron's (2000) "cultural arbitrary." No culture is "natural" but almost always appears to be so to those in it.

We now examine some of the more popular government and private sector antidotes to low or failing schools.

SOME CURRENT REFORM
EFFORTS AND THE BUNKUM AWARD

The Obama/Duncan critique for teacher preparation is threefold, based on the following: 1. Jobs of the future; 2. Education is the solution to inequities; and 3. The Baby-Boom generation retiring will bring about an unprecedented shortage of teachers. The Blueprint for Reform (U.S. Department of Education, 2010, March) states that university preparation does not prepare teachers to succeed in today's classrooms and universities are not selective enough on admissions, and the Blueprint is seeking strong models, urgently, to turn it all around.

The solutions offered are, for example, charter schools (ending the era of teacher unions) and Teach for America. These and other *strong models* are the hope for twenty-first-century schools.

The subtext of Teach for America, an alternative teacher certification program, is that a school can build a permanent solution on a model of teaching that is transitory. TFA is said "to be the rescue, for a minute" (Kain, 2010). TFA's role in improving urban education is to recruit Ivy League college graduates for a two-year classroom "adventure" in urban schools. Two years similar to the Peace Corps to enter urban schools that already suffer from high staff turnover doesn't make sense.

What interests does public education have in this experiment? For districts, it provides staff in hard-to-place, high-turnover schools for cheaper salaries.

One might speculate that, as with military service, TFA offers a future political club for privatization of education. Miner (2010) cites Linda Darling-Hammond's 2005 study that found "no instance where uncertified Teach for America teachers performed as well as standard certified teachers of comparable experience levels teaching in similar settings" (p. 28).

Equity and societal power positions from the elite to the marginalized continue to receive attention from the federal level. From the 1960s War on Poverty, education has been a focus on the national agenda. From a Nation at Risk in 1983 the politicalization of the public agenda moved to a position that both primary political parties, Republicans and Democrats, have tried to leverage to their advantage.

Federal Title I funds have been linked to Goals 2000, Reads First, No Child Left Behind, and the reauthorization of the ESEA Act of 2011. These mostly unfunded mandates from the federal government encourage states to adopt *voluntarily* national standards. The American Recovery and Reinvestment Act, ARRA, offers incentive grants to states and districts.

These grants focus on: educator quality, data systems, innovation among teachers, processes of evaluation, technology use, more rigorous core standards and assessments, and improvement of low-performing schools. The ARRA grants mandate assessment practices that evaluate *effectiveness* of teachers, principals, schools, and districts based heavily on student achievement scores arrived at from the testing of the national standards.

The primary focus for the Obama/Duncan Blueprint for Reform is the abiding belief in numbers, measurements, and assessments. Standardized testing, Kain (2010) believes, is like weighing cows to ensure the death of public education.

Of concern is the one-size-fits-all approach: all public schools without a clear focus on urban, rural, or suburban districts, with or without high levels of families in poverty. Title I funds have not worked precisely because once states received the money they "equitably" distributed the funds to all districts, rather than concentrating the funds within school settings that had more students with the most concerns.

Recently the U.S. Department of Education was awarded the Bunkum Award in 2010 for resting on "exceptionally disappointing low quality" research to support the Blueprint for Reform. The Bunkum Award was bestowed by the National Education Policy Center at the University of Colorado. The NEPC noted that the government "religiously avoided acknowledging or using the large body of high-quality research . . . that it had commissioned and published over the years" (Bunkum Awards, 2010, p. 1) despite the fact that they had said their recommended policies would be grounded in research.

Likewise, family and community ownership are not necessarily an incentive to ARRA. Equal is not equitable. Simmons (2010) believes the ARRA's approach *obscures* the differences among students: "English language learners, students with disabilities, recent immigrants, over-age and under-credited students . . . early parenthood students, childcare . . . previous incarceration, violence, health concerns, and other factors that contribute to the achievement gap and a lack of engagement" (p. 57).

Schools are but a node in a larger chain of agencies and organizations. Effective school leaders understand how to reach out, connect, and also at times how to be friendly critics of social practices that are detrimental to schools. How we build social capital within our city, state, and nation is just not the sole purview of the public schools.

The policy makers within the beltway and those professional organizations have for the last thirty years used public education for personal and professional gain. What has been lost (Gordon & Bridglall, 2005) is how public schooling prepares students to: 1) Contribute to civic life; 2) Form and strengthen families; 3) Value and contribute to the arts; and, 4) Respect local culture and traditions while becoming part of the mainstream.

These policy makers believe community-centered education reform can provide the political, social, and moral capital required to counter forces that derail and delay the succession of reforms tried since *Brown v. Board of Education.*

In the 2009 Programme for International Student Assessment (PISA) comparison, American students (Organization for Economic Co-operation and Development, 2010) ranked middle-of-the-road in some areas and higher in others for American fifteen-year-olds. This report, used widely to bash public schools, also notes that the top-reported schools are schools in countries that have high autonomy, respect teachers and principals, and are not competitively measured so as to compete for students.

DEVELOPING SOCIALLY JUST SCHOOLS

Socially just schools are earmarked by enlightened school leadership and strong community action. Marshall and Oliva (2010) describe school-community interactions through various modes of participation, involvement of local people, and the relationship of school and action to local community. The school-community interaction needs to be: 1) On real community interaction, not co-optation; 2) Actions for community integrated with the schools agenda; 3) Consultation for and with the community, cooperation with the community; 4) Co-learning with and by the community; and, 5) Collective action by the community (p. 310).

Leading, designing, and implementing a successful social justice coalition is difficult and demanding work (Marshall & Oliva, 2010, p. 323). The school leader must know how to propose alliances with police, foster care, healthcare, religious groups, and organizations (p. 325).

They posit that there are distinctions between a good leader and a social justice leader. They define the socially just leader as one who values diversity, ends pull-out programs, ensures that all students have access to the core curriculum, is responsive to differences due to wealth, is integrally intertwined with life in the community within the school, and whose professional development is culturally appropriate.

Recognizing that for persons of color social stratification is a fact of life is the lens the school leader must develop. Effective socially just leaders must learn ways to not perpetuate what nonwhite students have long faced: higher dropout rates and greater unemployment.

HEURISTICS FOR THE ACTIVIST LEADER

Heuristic 8: The public school pupil mix will continue to be even more diverse than it is today, calling into question the existing dominance of the Euro-American majoritarian cultural perspective on many fronts, from "core curriculums" to "standardized tests." All of the demographic trends concerning the racial and ethnic composition of the U.S. indicate the country is becoming more and more diverse. In fact, it is estimated that by the year 2050 whites will no longer be the majority. The largest gain will be from Hispanics, and minority children will become the majority by 2031 (Yen, 2009).

For years minority children have been at a disadvantage when they are immersed in a school culture that is alien and often incommensurable with their lived life experiences. Their lack of success in schools is due to this disadvantage as they drop out in larger numbers and as their alienation grows (MacLeod, 1987; Solomon, 1992).

Increasingly, the tension between the cultural perspectives of the once dominant majority Euro-American view will be called into question as to its propriety and relevance. For example, Au (2009) has indicated that standardized tests institutionalize inequality because it is a statistical impossibility for all students to reach 100 percent proficiency because standardized tests "require that a certain percentage of students fail in order to be considered valid and reliable" (Popham, 2001, as cited in Au, 2009, p. 138). Gibson (2001) has called high stakes testing "a form of regulated elitism" (as cited in Au, 2009, p. 139).

Heuristic 9: The profound quandary of African-American and Native American students in schools dominated by Euro-American cultural perspectives places them at extreme risk of alienation and failure. The dominant cultural perspective outlined by Boykin (1986) in this chapter places some minority students at an extreme disadvantage in the schools. An activist leader works to create awareness on the part of the faculty and support staff of this fundamental problem and works to ease the tensions involved.

One solution is to teach both cultures in the school and to make majoritarian students aware of their own cultural lenses in the process. An activist leader also works to create understanding that curriculum is biased if it does not question the cultural arbitrariness embedded within it, and so are tests and other educational materials and accompanying pedagogies if they are not interrogated as well.

Heuristic 10: Poverty is not a random variable among children and the inequality gap is growing in the U.S. The large repository of research and statistics continues to demonstrate that poverty does not embrace American school children as a random (or chance) variable. Rather, poverty impacts Americans disproportionately, that is, concentrating on African American, Native American, and Hispanic student populations in very great numbers.

Research shows that it is far more difficult for black families to remove themselves from poverty than white families (Hertz, 2005). Black families are much more likely to remain poor over several generations than white families. The income gap in the United States between rich and poor is expanding. It is the second highest of all countries in the world, behind only China (*The Economist*, 2011). This trend is profoundly troubling for the future of a democracy.

CONCLUSION

Barry (2005) believes that the political focus on individual responsibility avoids the government's responsibility: ". . . [a] new-born baby cannot possibly be responsible for the material social conditions into which it is born, and that whatever *decisions* a child may make for a number of years after that cannot be its responsibility" (p. 46).

Future actions are dependent on a variety of complex players: The federal government, which increasingly is seen as not supporting public education; the professional organizations marching states to the neo-liberal perspective; the accreditation bodies providing open access through accreditation to for-profits, etc. As Levin (2009) stated:

> The quest for educational equity is a moral imperative for a society in which education is a crucial determinant of life chances. Yet whether there is an economic return to the taxpayer for investing in educational justice is often not considered. (p. 5)

The challenges for activist leaders working in public schools is to continue to point out the inequities of punishing students for being poor and blaming them for the lack of cultural knowledge when they arrive at schools. Effective leaders understand that the form of cultural capital embraced by the schools is arbitrary and supported primarily through political power. No culture is right or wrong. Rather, cultures are different.

Explicit Leader Beliefs and Actions

1. Respect and understand family, home, and the cultures of your students: Leaders fundamentally respect the cultural backgrounds of their students and parents as not deficient

but distinctive. The public schools exist to serve and educate all the children of all the people. Understand that the more a specific culture is aligned with the Euro-American culture the more likely students will experience success, and the more students' lived cultural experiences are at odds with that culture, the more likely their success becomes problematic.

2. Some forms of student resistance to the school are a healthy sign of their protest, their desire not to be erased or have their cultural identities compromised: In a school where minority students perceive the school as being skewed toward white students, their opposition and resistance to the school can be associated with a desire to avoid having their distinctiveness erased (Fordham & Ogbu, 1986). Similarly, the creation and maintenance of a separate black cultural identity required African-American students to oppose school norms and to take out their frustrations on fellow minority students who did conform because they were "acting white" (Solomon, 1992, p. 4).

3. School leaders must create a student climate that does not require cultural identities to be erased in order for minority students to do well in schools. Student solidarity around cultural identities is required by them for survival "in a hostile, urban, street corner environment" (Solomon, 1992, p. 4). Punishing students for trying to survive in the world they live in is counterproductive.

Troubleshooting Guide

- Single programs will not turn around schools: A comprehensive approach, one that is culturally sensitive with all constituents, is required to ensure the particular programs chosen make sense for the students and community and reduce the feeling of alienation that some student sub-groups feel toward an institution which devalues them and their cultural identities.
- School culture is not neutral and favors some student groups over others in profound and totalizing ways: School culture, comprised of curriculum content, dominant pedagogy, assump-

tions about learning and the accepted cultural world view which lies behind all of them including teacher attitudes about students themselves, has to be unlocked carefully and with an eye to breaking the interconnecting parts so that when one's practice or belief is abandoned, it is not replaced with a corollary value or practice which is simply a new name for the old one.

- Student resistance to school culture and ways is an acquired (learned) response: Students do not initially come to school hating it. Learning that school is not a place for them or is inhospitable or indifferent to them and their background or potentialities puts students off and over time molds some of them into a defensive, negative, and hostile frame of mind. Turning around schools means taking on beliefs and practices that demean and devalue students. In order to do this successfully, activist leaders must become aware of how schools really work to disenfranchise some students and advantage others.

REFERENCES

Au, W. (2009). *Unequal by design: High-stakes testing and the standardization of inequality.* New York: Routledge.

Barry, B. (2005). *Why social justice matters.* Cambridge, UK: Polity Press.

Bourdieu, P., & Passeron, J. C. (2000). *Reproduction in education, society and culture,* 2nd ed. Thousand Oaks, CA: Sage.

Boykin, A. (1986). The triple quandary and the schooling of Afro-American children. In U. Neisser (ed.) *The school achievement of minority children: New perspectives* (pp. 57–92). Hillsdale, NJ: Lawrence Erlbaum Associates, Publishers.

Bunkum Awards. (2010). The "Good Enough for Government Award." Retrieved February 15, 2011, from http://nepc.colorado.edu/think-tank/bunkum-awards/2010.

Chang, H. (2010, September 15). Five myths about school attendance. *Education Week,* 30(3), p. 29.

Delgado-Gaitan, C. (1990). *Literacy for empowerment: The role of parents in children's education.* Bristol, PA: The Falmer Press.

Dolan, M. (2011, February 14). Crisis mode persists for Detroit schools. *The Wall Street Journal,* A5.

The Economist. (2011, January 22–28). Measuring inequality. 398 (8717), p. 8, in The Few: A special report on global leaders.

Enright, D. (2001). *The wicked wit of Winston Churchill.* London: Michael O'Mara Books Limited.

Fordham, S., & Ogbu, J. (1986). Black students' school success: Coping with the burden of acting white. *The Urban Review,* 13 (2), 281–297.

Freedland, J. (2007, May 9). Don't be fooled by Europe's mood. Globally, the left is reawakening. *The Guardian.*

Gibson, R. (2001). Outfoxing the destruction of wisdom. *Theory and Research in Social Education,* 29 (2), 308–329.

Gordon, E. W., & Bridglall, B. L. (2005). The challenge, context, and the preconditions of academic development at high levels. In E. W. Gordon, B. L. Bridglall, and A. S. Meroe (eds.), *Supplementary Education: The Hidden Curriculum of High Academic Achievement.* Lanham, MD: Rowman and Littlefield.

Hacker, J., & Pierson, P. (2010). *Winner-take-all politics: How Washington made the rich richer—and turned its back on the middle class.* New York: Simon & Schuster.

Hart, B., & Risley, T. R. (1995). *Meaningful differences in the everyday experience of young American children.* Baltimore, MD: Paul H. Brookes Publishing Co., pp. 132–133, 144–146.

Herrnstein, R., & Murray, C. (1994). *The bell curve.* New York: Free Press.

Hertz, T. (2005). Rags, riches and race: The intergenerational economic mobility of black and white families in the United States. In S. Bowles, H. Gintis, & M. Groves (eds.), *Unequal chances: Family background and economic success* (pp. 165–191). New York: Russell Sage Foundation and the Princeton University Press.

Irvin, G. (2008). *Super rich: The rise of inequality in Britain and the United States.* Malden, MA: Polity Press.

Kain, D. (2010). *Teacher preparation: Are universities making the needed changes?* A presentation at the annual Arizona School Administrators Superintendents and Higher Education Conference, Prescott, AZ, October 26.

Karrer, P. (2011, February 2). A letter to my president—the one I voted for. *Education Week,* 30 (19), 23.

Kincheloe, J. & Steinberg, S. (1997). Who said it can't happen here? In J. Kincheloe, S. Steinberg, & A. Gresson, *Measured lies: The bell curve examined* (pp. 3–47). New York: St. Martin's Press.

Levin, H. M. (2009). The economic payoff to investing in educational justice. *Educational Researcher,* 38(1), 5–20. doi:10.3102/0013189X08331192.

MacLeod, J. (1987). *Ain't no makin' it: Leveled aspirations in a low-income neighborhood.* Boulder, CO: Westview Press.

Marshall, C., & Oliva, M. (2010). *Leadership for social justice: Making revolutions in education,* 2nd ed. Boston, MA: Allyn & Bacon.

Maynor, P. (2011). Bourdieu's habitus and the educational achievement of North Carolina's American Indian students: An empirical investigation. Unpublished doctoral dissertation. University of North Carolina at Chapel Hill.

Miner, B. (2010). Looking past the spin. *Rethinking Schools,* 24(3), 24–33.

Mishel, L., Bernstein, J. & Allegretto, S. (2007). *The state of working America 2006/07.* Ithaca, NY: Economic Policy Institute, Cornell University Press.

Murray, C. (2005, September 29). The hallmark of the underclass. *The Wall Street Journal,* A18.

Norton-Smith, T. (2010). *The dance of person and place: One interpretation of American Indian philosophy.* Albany, NY: SUNY Press.

Organization for Economic Co-operation and Development (OECD). (2010). PISA 2009 results: Executive summary. Retrieved January 30, 2011, from www.oecd.org/dataoecd/34/60/46619703.pdf.

Organization for Economic Co-operation and Development (OECD) (2001). *Employment Outlook 2001.* Paris: OECD.

Papa [aka Papa-Lewis], R., & Fortune, R. (2002). *Leadership on purpose: Promising practices for African American and Hispanic students.* Thousand Oaks, CA: Corwin.

Popham, J. (2001). *The truth about testing: An educator's call to action.* Alexandria, VA: ASCD.

Ravitch, D. (2010). *The death and life of the great American school system: How testing and choice are undermining education.* New York: Basic Books.

Simmons, W. (2010, Winter). Urban education reform: Recalibrating the federal role. *Annenberg Institute for School Reform,* pp. 54–64.

Solomon, R. (1992). *Black resistance in high school: Forging a separatist culture.* Albany, NY: SUNY Press.

US Department of Education (2010). Blueprint for reform. Washington, DC: US Department of Education.

Vinovskis, M. (2009). *From a Nation at Risk to No Child Left Behind: National education goals and the creation of federal education policy.* New York: Teachers College Press.

Yen, H. (2009, December 17). Census: White majority to end by midcentury. *The Atlanta Journal-Constitution,* A13.

4

THE YIN AND YANG OF SUCCESSFUL SCHOOL TURNAROUNDS

Involving parents and the community means more than complying with federal or state mandates to get a rubber stamp for the school's agenda. It means sharing decision-making power with those who know the students best, the parents.

−anonymous urban public school teacher,
from Papa & Fortune, 2002

The ancient Chinese symbol of yin and yang is a wonderful metaphor for what it takes to be successful in turning around low-performing or failing schools. The yin and yang symbol is a circle with one side black and other white with dots in the center of each of the opposite color. What the symbol stands for is that while there are opposites, they stand together as part of a dynamic whole.

Both opposites are necessary for the whole to prosper and to work. For example, yin may symbolize advancement, while the yang stands for retreat. We think not only that the symbol is appropriate for turning around schools, but that what may appear to be opposite forces can actually be seen to be working together and that focusing only on one without the other presents a false picture of the challenges involved.

THE YIN: A FOCUS ON THE SCHOOL UNIT

We have focused much of our discussion thus far on the school site. The reason should be clear. Rarely do whole school districts fail. Even in very low-performing school districts one can usually find some schools which are acceptable. However, individual school units are deemed the ones who fail because the measures of success are all linked to the school site.

Over the years, the search for best practices in schools and best practices for leaders to exhibit has been fraught with difficulties. The effective schools movement of twenty-five years ago brought the inevitable question of the definition of effective. Is it test scores? Which ones? National standardized, state specific, textbook specific, etc.?

In addition, the effective schools data could never be used to predict success since the variables were only correlative. English (2002, Winter) has argued that the method of verifying the effective schools correlates was typical of some social science research practices that were elliptical and circular and provided no new theoretical or practical insights into that which was already known.

Such issues have not been resolved. Other concomitant issues were those of publisher, defined as part of specific reading, math, or social science texts; politically based "best" (e.g., immersion versus bilingual language programs, etc.); "Statistically significant" practices where sample sizes made the smallest of gains or program differences; "Significantly" better and best practices in context (For whom? Poor children, gifted children, etc.).

In 2002, the book *Leadership on Purpose: Promising Practices for African American and Hispanic Students* was published (Papa & Fortune, 2002) based on an intensive study of thirteen urban public schools which were high-achieving by California standards at the time (API = Academic Performance Index) and which were comprised of at least 63 percent to 97 percent (with an average across the schools of 84 percent) Mexican American and/or African American students, and high-poverty schools (average 53 percent).

The practices identified ran the gamut from specific skills given to students (e.g., teach and practice strategies throughout the year), through school-based practices (e.g., teachers know the standards and tie them to lesson plans) to district level practices (e.g., structured high expectations for everyone). The book and practices were widely used in districts similar to those used in the original study.

Continuing research over the years since the publication of *Leadership on Purpose: Promising Practices for African American and Hispanic Students* has tried to more clearly define and differentiate practices as they apply specifically to school leaders (most notably principals and superintendents). As well, the research has begun to yield results, pointing to those practices that are site- and/or student-specific (transient) versus those that apply to any leader in any context (intransient).

The most recent iteration of the original research in California has been with Arizona superintendents and principals. Both groups, through surveys and focus groups, have been asked to identify practices they see as critical to high-achieving students. That research has led to what Papa (2011) has defined as the "accoutrements" of leadership: the perspectives and outlooks concerning leadership developed through application and practice and which are descriptively *sewn* into one's persona as s/he develops into a fully fledged leader. The "accoutrements," discussed further in this chapter and in chapter 5, involve the following:

- Adult Learners: Leaders should know adult learners learn on a need-to-know basis (Papa & Papa, 2011).
- Human Agency: Leaders must have a varied repertoire of fair and just behaviors.
- Ignored Intended Skills: Leaders must be adept at listening, mentoring, and showing compassion.
- Intellectual Curiosity: Leaders must be curious. Curiosity is fairness in action as it asks "why" with no assigning of blame.
- Futurity: Leaders must be exposed to learning frames that go against the grain of current wisdom. Going against the grain may just be the best leader trait we can encourage.

- Imaginativeness: Creativity, inspiration, originality, resource-fulness, visionary, artistic, inventive, ingenious are the synonyms to imaginative leadership. Experience with good heart, an almost spiritual need to be of service for others; to be the hope for others; to help others be all they can be; to see the good in others is limited only by one's lack of imagination.

By accoutrements, Papa is referring to those aspects of leadership that go beyond the basic requirements of a leader's positional authority; the accessories *sewn* into one's persona, the perspectives and the bells and whistles that separate the truly effective leaders from the rest.

In the literature of leadership, the characteristics mentioned are often more abstract than specific. For example, we all talk of vision as if we know exactly what it means (e.g., lead by example, communicate, develop a sense of purpose, etc.). In training programs, we often focus on the basics required by administrators (legal issues, finance, school personnel, and curriculum) which are clearly necessary, but which some would argue are insufficient for leadership.

Thus, these are the basics for which the accoutrements are applied. While our definitions of leadership are often illusory, abstract, and subject to different interpretations, the training is tied to the basics: the federal and state specifics of a position that varies across sites, urban, rural, suburban, Northwest to Southeast and all differences in between.

When we talk about leadership, we often describe personal characteristics while simply stating that the specific tasks of the job are accomplished—but truly effective leadership goes beyond them. For example, in Arizona a Rodel Exemplary Principal is described as someone who "fosters strong leadership in high-need schools" (Faller, 2011, January 23, p. B 4). This expectation clearly goes beyond a simple description of managerial tasks.

This projected yin and yang is often confused as the dichotomy of leadership versus management. We often say that one can be a good manager, but may *not* be a good leader. This is a false dichotomy in that it can be argued that good leaders need the basics of management for the leadership qualities to be exhibited (English, 2008a, p. 13).

In a recent focus group of twelve elementary/middle school principals (three identified as Rodel Exemplary Principals 2009–2011), several district-level administrators and the superintendent can serve as an example of the accoutrements in practice-specific skills that could be learned and transferred across personnel and districts. The session started with a straightforward prompt that asked what makes this school exemplary as noted by the State of Arizona. The initial response from a principal, seconded by all, was the established culture focused on student learning and collegial support.

When asked for specificity, what emerged were specific practices that promoted that culture. For example, at district meetings communication is emphasized, with each administrative team member sharing assessments of his/her school, using data to talk about achievement, student issues, parent issues, etc. (*Human Agency*, and *Ignored Intended Skills*). Their focus is on where they are now and where they want to go (*Futurity*).

In addition, these principals were encouraged by their superintendent to seek literature on relevant topics and provided a budget to explore alternative solutions to student learning outcomes (*Intellectual Curiosity*). They undergo the same professional development as the teachers with respect to instructional tools (*Adult Learners*) and are encouraged and supported to build personal relationships with their students, staffs, and parents to make it easier and more productive in the work environment (*Human Agency*). They spend two days a week as instructional leaders, visible in classrooms and active in instruction (*Imaginativeness*).

During those two days of each week, the superintendent doesn't involve them in administration, except in emergencies (*Adult Learners*). In sum, these public school leaders feel professional and responsible. It is clear that the basics of management (budgets, discipline, personnel, etc.) are "givens" rather than purely administrative priorities that are their only tasks.

As noted previously, this is where the accoutrements (Papa, 2011) take a first step in that direction. The assumption is that anyone going for the superintendency has mastered the basics through training and/or experience at the principalship level. Then the specifics of accoutrements kick in: understanding the adult learner; sense of human agency (fair and just behaviors towards all); ignored intended skills (listening, mentoring, reflecting); intellectual curiosity; futurity; and imaginativeness. The work continues to more specifically define these skills and their ability to be amplified and transferred through application and practice.

These accoutrements were developed from an extensive review of the literature and ten years of empirical data starting with *Leadership on Purpose: Promising Practices for African American and Hispanic Students* (2002) and continuing through recent studies of successful schools.

The Papa and Fortune (2002) and Papa (2011) findings were also mirrored in other leadership studies internationally. For example, a study of ten outstanding leaders in and out of education conducted by Cranston and Ehrich (2007) in Australia revealed very similar results though described in slightly different terms. These are shown synoptically in table 4.1 below.

It is clear from a comparison of these two studies by a team of different researchers in two different settings that:

- Leaders are self-constructed and not born. They are the sum total of their life experiences.
- Effective leadership is centered in a moral values base, which also is an anchor for the leader's vision
- Leadership is about working with and through others, drawing the best out of the people with whom one works. It's not about "me"; rather it is about "us."
- While leaders work with a sense of purpose based on a commitment to their ideals, they remain open-minded intellectually and curious about how things work and what moves people, and can change their minds when the facts don't match the situation.

Table 4.1. A Comparison of the Papa Accoutrements of Leadership to Lessons of Leadership

Characteristic	Papa Accoutrements	Cranston & Ehrich Leadership of Lessons	Commentary
Leadership of adult learners	Leadership preparation is grounded in theory and practice and occurs on a "need-to-know" basis	Formal and informal learning is critical to leadership development	Learning to be a leader should be multidimensional and involve more than formal course work in a university or agency setting
Human agency	Focus on the totality of human existence, rejection of a "one-size-fits-all" mental model	Leadership is values-driven; it ought to be about seeking equity and tolerance	Leadership is concerned with human existence and social justice and working towards a better world; it is a moral endeavor
Ignored but intended skills	Leadership skills are not all reducible to discrete behaviors; a rejection of reductionism	Life forces, experiences, and opportunities explored are fundamental to leadership development	Leadership is more than the technical acquisition of discrete skill sets; it is a value defined and driven enterprise enacted with and through followers
Intellectual curiosity	Leaders should be curious about all aspects of leading and learning	Leadership is a journey of discovery, seeking answers to intriguing questions	Closed minds do not see leadership as open-ended and therefore are not interested in the unanswered questions; leadership is quest
Futurity	Leadership involves multiple frames of knowing and understanding in order to grasp a future which is different than the status quo	A quest to effect change for a better future is the critical challenge for leaders	Being able to more fully understand the challenges of the future requires the ability to reframe the field
Imaginativeness	This facet of leadership is also connected to creativity, originality, and inspiration	Leadership draws on creativity, risk taking and a capacity to lead and develop others in collaborative work	Leaders are required to have a vision, but visions are anchored to imagination and creativity

- Because leadership is a projection of self, the first lesson of leadership is to understand one's self. A leader cannot lead without understanding what motivates himself/herself.
- Leadership is about a journey taken with others and lived with and through others. It is not a destination but a quest.
- Leadership involves the total human being: not just the rational side, but the emotional and feeling side as well.

If we are to move from the concept of "leaders are born not made," then we must more clearly define exemplary practices for leadership. Can a variety of personality types be successful leaders? Absolutely, *if* the trait or personality isn't immune to change, and if the individual embraces the aspects derived from the two studies cited here.

We also must differentiate those practices that are contextually specific from those which transcend a specific setting. In addition, there are those leadership actions which are interdependent for their success upon the reactions of individuals in a specific setting. The effectiveness of these leadership actions cannot be considered apart from the response of others in the setting.

Then there are those which are independent of such actions, though we must confess we can't think of very many of them. For example, let us take a rather mundane decision by a school principal to have his school painted. Such a decision might not encounter any reaction, unless the painting went on during school time and was particularly smelly or not in keeping with the color of the rest of the building. Given that the painting was not intrusive and happened on the weekends or at night, no one would care very much about it.

Most administrative actions are indeed reactive, that is, someone in a building is going to be impacted in some way by them and will react. For this reason accoutrements must be seen as something above and beyond the core skills rather than superficial characteristics or phrases such as "acts like a leader."

THE YANG: UNDERSTANDING THE SCHOOL
SITE IS PART OF A LARGER SCHOOL SYSTEM

Few things in American education are more integral to the development of the nation than the *school district*. Knezevich (1975) remarked, "The district system is an American invention. It was well suited to a pioneer culture where localism was cherished and democracy a passion" (p. 205). Originally individual schools were connected to villages and towns. However, the distance involved and often-difficult terrain to traverse made it challenging for children in the rural areas to attend town schools. So some system had to be created whereby children in more remote areas could be educated.

At first the system of having teachers move about in the geographical areas was tried. These wandering pedagogues would spend some time in remote areas teaching the children and then moving on to others. But the time periods in between such schooling could be two to three years, resulting in the fact that some "children enjoyed very long vacations" (Knezevich, 1975, p. 206). The solution to this problem was to create an organizational/administrative unit that included both the town and rural schools, and thus the creation of the American school district.

The school district also suited the attitudes of many of the pioneering people who moved West. These people "were independent and ruggedly individualistic, and they cherished their liberties. They were opposed to giving up any rights of self-determination, even to their own township or state governments" (Grieder, Pierce, & Rosenstengel, 1961, p. 6). The result was the proliferation of school districts.

Even at the time thoughtful viewers of the educational scene perceived some of the downsides of school districts. The putative "father of American education," Horace Mann, considered "the school district as the worst curse of American education" (Grieder, Pierce, & Rosenstengel, 1961, p. 5). But it should be remembered that Mann struggled against the voices of localism much of his professional life in imposing his educational reforms which required the power of centralization (Messerili, 1971).

Almost from the beginning one of the evils of localism was that school committees or boards varied the tax rates from district to district, and this uneven level of monetary support for schools began the trend of unequal educational opportunity that took nearly two centuries to redress in state and federal courts (Knezevich, 1975, p. 207).

The school district remains firmly a fixture in American education because it is "(1) a political entity, or civil subdivision of the state; (2) a legal entity, or quasi-municipal corporation; (3) a geographical entity; (4) a social institution; and (5) an educational entity" (Knezevich, 1975, p. 207). The number of school districts reached a high of 127,000 in the early 1930s (Grieder, Pierce, & Rosenstengel, 1961, p. 5), but had shrunk to approximately 16,850 in 2001 (NCES, 2001).

As the cities grew in population so did the size and pupil enrollment of school districts (Tyack, 1975, pp. 28–72). Today, 23 percent of the nation's school districts are represented by the 100 largest ones. They enroll 40 percent of the minority students in the country and 30 percent of the economically disadvantaged students (NCES, 2001). The crisis of school effectiveness is most acute in the cities, though a different sort of crisis exists in rural areas.

While school bureaucracies bloomed and began to become controlled by professional elites, management problems were also becoming evident. School board micromanagement was a consistent problem then as now. Ayers' (1916) study of the Cleveland Public Schools found him recommending that "the board conduct a careful study of its own activities with the purpose of relieving itself so far as possible of the transaction of detailed routine business" (p. 92).

Over fifty years later, Rogers' (1968) detailed study of the bureaucratic dilemmas of the New York City Public Schools indicated that that board of education "is a prime example of the short-range oriented, reactive, fire-fighting organization, and this acts to preclude the central board and superintendent from playing an effective role in managing future changes" (p. 396).

These well-documented problems with highly bureaucratic centralized school systems have pushed many reformers to abandon any attempt to change them at all. Instead they have opted to split individual school sites away from centralized systems and bypass the controversy between centralization and de-centralization altogether (Reyes, 2006). This results in an extreme form of site-based management very popular in the 1990s. However, extreme site-based management is largely dysfunctional in highly centralized systems of standardized testing utilized by most states in assessing school accountability (English & Steffy, 2011, pp. 289–308).

The Council for Great City Schools commissioned a case study of selected urban school systems in the U.S. that had demonstrated an overall trend of improved student achievement for at least three years and had decreased the gap between white and minority students. In addition, these systems were making greater progress than their other urban counterparts and they were geographically typical of urban school systems.

The study results were released in 2002 (Snipes, Doolittle, & Herlihy). The school districts were Sacramento, California; Charlotte-Mecklenburg, North Carolina; Houston Independent School District, Texas; and the Chancellor's District in New York City. Each of these systems had been characterized as having endured political conflict; a largely inexperienced teaching staff; low expectations and the absence of a rigorous curriculum; lack of instructional coherence; high student mobility; and an unsatisfactory set of business operations.

The Council for Great City Schools study produced nine strategies that the selected school districts employed to meet the criteria for being selected. These are shown in table 4.2 set against the implications for impacting low-performing schools situated within a school system as most are.

As can be seen from table 4.2, low-performing schools cannot simply be roped off from the rest of the school district. What is crucial for turning around low-performing schools is to re-connect them to the system, re-establish the flow of resources and enhance them,

Table 4.2. A Comparison of the *Strategies of Success* & *Turnaround Schools*

Area	What CGCS Successful Districts Did in Strategies of Success	The Importance to Turnaround Schools
Establishing a focus	Improved student achievement was established as the singular most important goal with a specific timetable created with defined consequences; curriculum was aligned with state standards and these were translated into instructional practices.	Especially for secondary schools who are dependent upon feeder schools to provide their students with the requisite skills prior to entrance, creating internal consistency and vertical connectivity is crucial for success among all schools, especially if pupil mobility is high. Only the school system can create aligned system-wide curriculum (English & Steffy, 2001). This ensures that any individual school will be connected to others so that prerequisite skills are taught prior to entrance. These, in turn, are aligned with state standards and tests.
Creating viable accountability systems	Systems of accountability for district and school leadership were put into place that exceeded state requirements.	Leaders have to lead by example. They can't ask others to be accountable if they are not.
Intervention sites	Successful districts focused on the lowest-performing schools and some provided additional resources to them.	Low-performing schools cannot be treated like all other schools. They have special needs and issues which must become a priority for the larger school system and will most likely require additional attention and resources.
Curriculum development	System-wide curriculum was created with matching instructional approaches rather than allowing each school to select its own.	The creation of an aligned system-wide curriculum ensures that students will be taught what is tested in state accountability systems (English, 2004, 2006, 2008b).

Professional development	Professional development was focused on selected system-wide objectives for consistent implementation district-wide.	Focused professional development is connected to improving low achievement because that is situated in successive systems of achievement defined by the district and the state.
Classroom reforms	Successful school systems drove reforms into the classroom by ensuring the central office was supporting them in the schools.	Central office support is crucial to turning around low-performing schools. Central office staff cannot treat all schools alike because they are not.
Use of data in decision making	Successful school districts define and utilize systems of data to inform decision making.	Low-performing schools require constant attention to the most important indicators that they are making progress along the desired or required instruments of measurement.
Reform focus	The CGCS successful districts initiated their reforms at the elementary schools instead of trying to fix everything.	The district must establish priorities if they expect results. They cannot fix everything.
Instructional focus	At the middle and high school levels CGCS districts focused almost exclusively on instruction in reading and math.	Reading and math become priorities because these are most often the measures used to assess progress.

ensure competent leadership in them, and focus staff development on school measures that are aligned with system-wide measures.

Low-performing schools are not simply isolated failures. Rather they represent *school system failures.* Fixing low-performing schools means fixing the school systems in which they are embedded. While certain actions can be taken which are independent of the school system to improve school site operations such as attendance and disciplinary procedures, the importance of curriculum alignment and instructional coherence are created on a system-wide basis.

Ultimately successful school turnarounds mean changing things at the central office. In this respect, low-performing schools are really just a symptom of school district dysfunctionality and faulty decision-making. Examples of failed system-wide school reforms occurred in the San Diego City Schools under the superintendency of non-educator Alan Bersin, and the New York City Schools under mayoral control of Michael Bloomberg who similarly brought in Joel Klein, a non-educator (Ravitch, 2010, pp. 47–92).

Non-educators have a low regard for democratic participation via school boards and teacher associations or unions. They see them as barriers and obstacles. A prime example is former IBM CEO Lou Gerstner, who said:

> When I took over IBM I found I had 81 profit centers. Oh my God: How am I going to create change with 81 profit centers? How'd you like to create change with 16,000 profit centers? These organizations stand in the way of what we want to do. (Gerstner, 2008, p. R9)

The reference by Gerstner to sixteen thousand profit centers is to the remaining number of school boards in America. It is clear from his comment that elected or appointed school boards "stand in the way" of what he and other business types think will improve schools. Their view is that a heavy-handed, top-down, authoritarian management style is the proper one to reform school districts when this is exactly what has characterized ineffective school district management in the past (Cuban, 1976; 2004).

In a rebuke of this portrait of successful educational management, Louis and Wahlstrom (2011) surveyed over 8,000 principals and teachers in 164 schools within a random sample of nine states that included all types of school districts. They found that the key to altering a school culture was *shared* or *distributed leadership*, not the "superman" or "lone ranger" image pushed by the popular media and business leaders.

Most disturbing of the views of how to change school districts is the disdain that business leaders have for not only accountability, because there is less public accountability under their models for change than before, but the intolerance for dissent of any kind. In reflecting on the control of the New York City Schools by Mayor Bloomberg, Ravitch (2010) wrote:

> It solves no problems to exclude parents and the public from important decisions about education policy or to disregard the educators who work with students daily. Public education is a vital institution in our democratic society, and its governance must be democratic, open to public discussion and public participation. (p. 91)

The relationship between turning schools around and the larger school district is profound and long lasting. Most schools cannot do it alone because the definition of "failing" is usually one that is applied from a system of standardized testing that is external to any individual school.

Systematic testing has marked some schools as pretty dismal places or, to coin a popular term, "dropout factories" (Duke & Jacobson, 2011, p. 34). While there may be much disagreement about how such schools are identified in the first place, that is, the morality or wisdom of establishing certain benchmarks over others, the criteria that designated a school as "failing" or "low-performing" has to be the same ones that are used to become "successful" as long as schools remain in that system.

An analogy might be that if you are in a game and want to come out a winner, you can't change the rules only for yourself. For a winner to be claimed, the same rules have to apply to all players, otherwise being a "winner" has no meaning.

The bottom line is that it takes understanding of system dynamics and competent leaders in the central office to make things happen at schools. These are among the most important heuristics learned from what we know so far.

HEURISTICS FOR THE ACTIVIST LEADER

Heuristic 11: School leadership success is intimately connected to school district leadership success. While it may be convenient and even romantic to think about turning schools around in isolation, an individual principal and his/her faculty can only do so much in isolation. S/he will require increased resource support, perhaps some waivers from larger school system policies, regulations, and practices, and strong political support when the times get rough as they inevitably will (Duke & Jacobson, 2011).

The commitment of the central office to their low-performing schools has to be manifest in "a commitment by the board and the superintendent to work together collaboratively, to candidly assess the strengths and weaknesses of the district, to put aside issues which do not impact achievement and to build community support for their plans" (Snipes, Doolittle & Herlihy, 2002, p. 63). There is an increasing awareness that superintendent stability is one of the cornerstones of success in turning schools around.

Heuristic 12: District leaders must face down pressures to treat all the schools the same in spite of their performance. There are enormous pressures on school district leaders to treat all the schools the same. Making exceptions without the buffer of a federal or state law for various exceptionalities is politically dangerous. When more funds flow to schools serving children from the lower classes, the politically powerful elites who normally exercise control may exert resistance and a backlash occurs. There can be an expressed fear that somehow if "those children" succeed, "our children" will not enjoy the cultural and educational advantages to which they are *entitled*.

Despite the rhetoric to the contrary, not everyone wants all children to do well in the schools, especially if it means that limited resources are redirected to those perceived not to be the same or *deserving*. It takes great courage for district leaders to confront these forces and pressures and often boards are representative of those class-centered interests.

Heuristic 13: The creation of an effectively aligned curriculum within a centralized testing program is a school district responsibility, while differentiated instruction is a school site responsibility. The key to improving scores on standardized tests of accountability rests on curriculum alignment (English, 2004; 2006; 2008b, 2010) and differentiated instruction (Thousand, Villa & Nevin, 2007). While curriculum alignment is a central responsibility, differentiated instruction is a school unit responsibility (Ward, 2004, p. 10).

Schools and school district personnel must share in the blame and/or the success of their efforts. If the curriculum to be tested is not taught, it doesn't matter if instruction is differentiated. However, if an aligned curriculum is not taught well and differentiated by critical differences in learners and learning styles, it will similarly not be as effective as it might be otherwise.

Heuristic 14: While school leadership involves learning, it is actually acquired (i.e., *an act of accoutering*) through development and practice. The "accoutrements" of leadership are not simply discrete skills, though some skills are part of being accoutered. The word *accoutrement* was borrowed from Middle French in 1596 and is traced back to the Renaissance Latin "accosturare," which meant to arrange or to sew something (Barnhart,1995, p. 6). In contemporary terms it means an article of equipment or dress which is acquired. Used in the research performed for this book, it refers to perspectives and outlooks concerning leadership developed through application and practice and which are descriptively *sewn* into one's persona as s/he develops into a fully fledged leader.

We fully believe leaders are made and not born. They develop and learn, make mistakes, and continue developing. We don't believe in traits because that would connote some sort of genetic origination. Leaders come to leadership and develop themselves. In the words of Warren Bennis (1989), "Leaders have nothing but themselves to work with" (p. 47).

CONCLUSION

While it is romantic to think about a lone Don Quixote riding into the wasteland of a low-performing or failing school and turning it around with Herculean efforts, it is hugely misleading. The successful leader of a turnaround school understands that what is involved in this type of makeover is nothing less than a "whole scale change in the culture and climate of an ongoing institution and it will lead to a confrontation of those social classes who have set up schools to perpetuate their continued dominance in the larger socio-political world" (Bolton, 2011, p. 224).

We have seen successful educational leaders and unsuccessful ones. We've worked for both kinds. What we do know is that while individual leadership is undoubtedly important, if it doesn't become collaborative, distributed, and shared, it will fail and fall.

Papa (2011) has developed the terminology of leadership "accoutrements" to differentiate between these two basic sets of educational leaders. We believe they contain a more fluid and dynamic picture of how leaders develop and what they develop into than the static models which undergird most of the standards for educational leaders from which we prepare them today (Papa, 2011, pp. 195–209).

Explicit Leader Beliefs and Actions

1. Your persona matters: Understand that you must continually throughout your career reflect and examine who you are. How you practice your craft reflects what your perspectives are, and your outlook is *sewn* into your persona.

2. Remain intellectually curious and imaginative: Going against the grain is only possible if you remain curious and can imagine a better school practice. What little one can control from outside sources is countered in one's enormous capacity to rethink, refocus and reflect on how to make a difference in students' lives.

Troubleshooting Guide

- Connect failing schools to failures of the school system: Most failing schools, especially in urban school districts, are part of a school system. Such schools should not be treated as though they were simply a bad apple in the barrel. In this case, one has to look at the barrel that contains the apples.
- A failing school is a school system failure for the simple reason that the control of resources, the provision of selecting competent leaders and teachers, aligning a curriculum to the extant assessment system, is a school system responsibility. What is a local school's responsibility is how the resources are applied and the extent to which instruction is successfully differentiated.
- Leadership is an acquired mantle which is sewn together from past experiences: The notion of leadership "accoutrements" is a blend between acquired habits learned through experience, and some habits of mind which are also acquired such as intellectual curiosity and imaginativeness. Educational leaders traffic in a base of moral values because the content of schooling represents an arbitrary choice of many possible "cultures." What supports that base is the dominant value system of the political elites who control schooling in any given culture (Bourdieu & Passeron, 2000). Part of the issue with low-performing schools is that typically the students they are supposed to be educating are from those segments of society who are not from the dominant elite culture. They are at an immediate and continuing disadvantage in a curriculum that

is tightly aligned with elite knowledge, language, and cultural capital. To change schooling so that it does something different will require a "metanoia," that is, "a mental revolution, a transformation of one's whole vision of the social world" or at least a new "gaze" (Bourdieu & Wacquant, 1992: as cited in Bolton, 2011, p. 223).

REFERENCES

Ayers, L. (1916). *Cleveland education survey: School organization and administration.* Philadelphia, PA: Fell Printers.

Barnhart, R. (1995). *The Barnhart concise dictionary of etymology.* New York: HarperCollins.

Bennis, W. (1989). *On becoming a leader.* Cambridge, MA: Perseus Books.

Bolton, C. (2011). Metanoia in educational leadership: An alternative perspective for school leadership. In F. English (ed.), *The Sage handbook of educational leadership,* 2nd ed. (pp. 223–229). Thousand Oaks, CA: Sage.

Bourdieu, P., & Passeron, J. C. (2000). *Reproduction in education, society and culture, 2nd ed.* London, UK: Sage.

Bourdieu, P., & Wacquant, L. (1992). *An invitation to reflexive sociology.* Cambridge, UK: Polity Press.

Cranston, N., & Ehrich, L. (2007). *What is this thing called leadership?* Brisbane, Australia: Australian Academic Press.

Cuban, L. (1976). *Urban school chiefs under fire.* Chicago: University of Chicago Press.

Cuban, L. (2004). *The blackboard and the bottom line.* Cambridge, MA: Harvard University Press.

Duke, D., & Jacobson, M. (2011, February). Tackling the toughest turnaround—low-performing high schools. *Phi Delta Kappan, 92* (5). 34–38.

English, F. (2010). *Deciding what to teach and test: Developing, aligning, and leading the curriculum,* 2nd ed. Thousand Oaks, CA: Corwin Press.

English, F. (2008a). *The art of educational leadership: Balancing performance and accountability.* Thousand Oaks, CA: Sage.

English, F. (2008b, March/April). The curriculum management audit: Making sense of organizational dynamics and paradoxes in closing the achievement gap. *Edge, 3* (4).

English, F. (2006, January). The good, the bad, and the ugly: Exploring the power of the curriculum audit. *School Business Affairs*, 72 (1), 11–14.

English, F. (2004, September). Confronting the achievement gap: Quick fixes versus lasting change. *School Business Affairs*, 70 (8), pp. 25–27.

English, F. (2002, Winter). Cutting the gordian knot of educational administration: The theory-practice gap. *UCEA Review*, 44 (1), pp. 1–3.

English, F., & Steffy, B. (2011). Curriculum leadership: The administrative survival skill in a test-driven culture and a competitive educational marketplace. In F. English (ed.), *The Sage handbook of educational leadership*, 2nd ed. (pp. 289–308). Thousand Oaks, CA: Sage.

Faller, M. B. (2011, January 23). Making leadership shine: Award-winning principal emphasizes parent interaction, "community" feel. *The Arizona Republic: Education focus on Rodel Exemplary Principals*, p. B4.

Gerstner, L. (2008, November 24). Failing our children. *The Wall Street Journal*, p. R9.

Grieder, C., Pierce, T., & Rosenstengel, W. (1961). *Public school administration*, 2nd ed. New York: The Ronald Press Company.

Knezevich, S. (1975). *Administration of public education*, 3rd ed. New York: Harper & Row.

Louis, K., and Wahlstrom, K. (2011, February). Principals as cultural leaders. *Phi Delta Kappan*, 95 (5), 52–56.

Messerili, J. (1971). *Horace Mann*. New York: Alfred A. Knopf.

NCES, National Center for Educational Statistics. (2001, October). *Characteristics of the 100 largest public elementary and secondary districts in the United States: 1999–2000*. Washington, DC.

Papa, R. (2011). Standards for educational leaders: Promises, paradoxes, and pitfalls. In F. English (ed.), *The Sage handbook of educational leadership: Advances in theory, research, and practice*, 2nd ed. (pp. 195–209). Thousand Oaks, CA: Sage.

Papa [aka Papa-Lewis], R., & Fortune, R. (2002). *Leadership on purpose: Promising practices for African American and Hispanic students*. Thousand Oaks, CA: Corwin.

Papa, R., & Papa, J. (2011). Leading adult learners: Preparing future leaders and professional development of those they lead. In R. Papa (Ed.) *Technology leadership for school improvement*. Thousand Oaks, CA: Sage Publications.

Ravitch, D. (2010). *The death and life of the great American school system: How testing and choice are undermining education*. New York: Basic Books, Inc.

Reyes, A. (2006). Decentralization/centralization controversy. In F. English (ed.), *Encyclopedia of educational leadership and administration* (pp. 267–271). Thousand Oaks, CA: Sage.

Rogers, D. (1968). *110 Livingston Street: Politics and bureaucracy in the New York City school system.* New York: Random House.

Snipes, J., Doolittle, F., & Herlihy, C. (2002). *Foundations for success: Case studies of how urban school systems improve student achievement.* Council for Great City Schools.

Thousand, J., Villa, R., & Nevin, A. (2007). *Differentiating instruction: Collaborative planning and teaching for universally designed learning.* Thousand Oaks, CA: Corwin Press.

Tyack, D. (1975). *The one best system: A history of American urban education.* Cambridge, MA: Harvard University Press.

Ward, R. (2004). *Improving achievement in low-performing schools: Key results for school leaders.* Thousand Oaks, CA: Corwin-Press.

5

SOCIALLY JUST
ACTIVIST LEADERS
TO TURN
AROUND SCHOOLS

Principals agree, "You need to be in the classroom to see what's going on—give feedback."

–anonymous urban public school principal,
from Papa & Fortune, 2002

Traditional models of leadership using outdated ideas of management are not likely to turn around underperforming or failing schools. A recent study reported in *Education Week* identified 2,025 chronically low-performing schools in ten states and indicated that: (1) only 1 percent "had improved enough five years later to exceed their states' average academic performance and fewer than 10 percent had broken out of the lowest 25 percent of schools in their states" (Sparks, 2011, p. 5) and; (2) there was no difference in this result between regular public schools and charter schools.

By outdated concepts of management we are referring to the characteristics of what Mintzberg (1983) has termed the "machine bureaucracy" which "is a structure with an obsession—namely control" (p. 167). Mintzberg (1983) indicates that this obsession is reflected in two central facts. The first is that every form of uncertainty is eliminated from the tasks of the organization. This is the reason for a fetish regarding standardized procedures and work rules. The second fact is that since the work is precisely defined, conflict is rife within such bureaucracies as human beings struggle to maintain a semblance of their autonomy and dignity within themselves.

Autonomy is the last thing the managers of machine bureaucracies desire because it is the source of work variance. Variance is clearly an obstacle to control and thinking about the work is not allowed by the workers. The father of the machine bureaucracy, Frederick Taylor, once lambasted a subordinate by telling him, "I don't want to hear anything more from you. You haven't got any brains, you haven't got any ability—you don't know anything . . . keep out of my way" (Kanigel, 1997, p. 354).

Machines act "without thought or emotion and without a guiding intelligence" (Lumby & English, 2010, p. 22), and the impact of employing machine metaphors to describe improving schools is counterproductive to their becoming more effective. Humans are not machines and never will be.

To deal with the phenomenon of worker individuality and initiative screwing up elaborate designed systems of work, a great deal of effort has to go into systems of surveillance and conformance to deal with conflict. Rather than flushing conflicts into the open to try and resolve them, managers in machine bureaucracies most often choose to suppress conflict through rigid work supervisory procedures that enforce compliance and conformance.

Tying teacher monetary increases to standardized test scores is one way to enforce machine bureaucratic rules. These are at the heart of the neo-liberal efforts to "reform" public education (Rhee, 2011).

Other ways resistance is suppressed lie in the form of standardized curriculum, such as the common core curriculum and the use of pacing charts to engage in rigid time management and new procedures for teacher supervision. Machine bureaucracies assume that teachers are interchangeable parts and that students must be standardized as the raw input for the machine to operate efficiently.

The whole apparatus has been called an example of *hyper-rationalization* by Wise (1979) in which he noted increasing centralization of educational decisions based on "established rules and procedures; scientific management techniques . . . adopted to increase efficiency; and goals . . . specified in measurable outcomes" (p. 47) with the result of "more bureaucratic overlay without attaining the intended policy objectives" (pp. 47–48).

Rigidity and routinization are the twin thrusts of leadership efforts in a machine bureaucracy. They are antithetical to substantive and sustained school improvement because of the simple fact that the more effective instruction becomes, the more differences exist in the students to which teachers must make exceptions within a curriculum and a work environment that eschews exceptions and has been developed to avoid them.

The rock on which machine bureaucracies are founded in education is the observation that human beings are not standardized, though they can be treated as though they were. This lack of fundamental differentiation lies at the heart of what we believe to be *the achievement gap*, organizing education as though every student is the same when they are not.

LEADING WITH THE HEART AND MIND

It was Mahatma Gandhi who once observed, "If you want something really important to be done, you must not merely satisfy the reason, you must move the heart also" (Iyer, 1973, p. 287). Leaders who turn schools around have to be "complete" principals, ones who are good at data analysis, and especially with matters of the heart. The reason is not hard to understand. For schools to become more effective places, they must become fairer places for all students, for as Bernstein (1996) observed,

> There is likely to be an unequal distribution of images, knowledges, possibilities, and resources that will affect

the rights of participation, inclusion, and individual en-
hancement of groups of students. It is highly likely that
the students who do not receive these rights in school
come from social groups who do not receive these rights
in society. (p. 8)

In her research regarding good high schools for which she won an
award from AERA (American Education Research Association) Sara
Lawrence-Lightfoot (1983) noted that

a final way of judging institutional goodness for students
is to observe the regard and treatment of the weakest
members. In each of these portraits [of good high schools]
we see a strong institutional concern for saving lost souls
and helping students who are most vulnerable. (p. 349)

In fact, Lawrence-Lightfoot (1983) capped her description by assert-
ing that "good schools are places where students are seen as people
worthy of respect" (p. 350).

Perhaps more than other types of educational environments, poor
or failing schools to be turned around require "complete" leaders.
These "complete" leaders not only have the intellectual and concep-
tual skills to direct complex organizations, but also understand the
human needs and problems in which their schools are embroiled.
They know that turning around schools involves not only master-
ing technical, and managerial skills, but also that it requires the
intangible work of empathy, imagination, understanding, curiosity,
modeling inspiration, and so on.

An example of an "incomplete leader" is the story of Columbia Secondary School founder Dr. Maldonado-Rivera. Initially seen as visionary, spontaneous, a Svengali, and especially charismatic, controversy
soon developed. He was fired in his fourth year. Why? Charisma is
not enough. Creating a school is not too difficult, especially if you are
viewed as charismatic: He began by sending a note out to parents that
said: "Come build a school with me" (Virshup, January 16, 2011, p. 27).

Keeping a school running is much more difficult. A leader's
personal charm, manifested in influence over others, is not enough

if that is all there is. It is not enough because it soon becomes apparent that without empathy and respect for others—such as not providing a translator at meetings with large numbers of Spanish-only–speaking parents or an understanding of how to ensure safety so a student does not drown during a field trip—does not model inspiration.

Balancing books and transparency of money usage was also not a forte of this "incomplete" leader, nor was school discipline. A "complete leader" must have a personal public life that is transparent, respect for one's teachers, budget and safety management, curricular knowledge, and other attributes. Again, charisma is not enough.

More will be said about these "complete" leader accoutrements in this chapter. For schools to work for all students they must become fairer places, that is, socially just places; for as a large cadre of sociologists have long noted in their research, schools are mostly places where the weakest members of society are dealt with most callously, inhumanely, and disrespectfully (Bernstein, 1996; Bourdieu & Passeron, 2000).

SOCIALLY JUST EDUCATIONAL LEADERS: THE CHALLENGE

A socially just educational leader cannot be oblivious to the larger American social structure of rather deep inequalities which exist in it. The American social structure exhibits huge disparities in income and, correspondingly, political power.

The gap between the rich and poor in America is the second highest of any country in the world, second only to Brazil (*The Economist*, 2006). Hacker & Pierson (2010) refer to the growing gap as the "hyper-concentration of income" and they cite that the top 1 percent's share of national income expanded from about 8 percent in 1974 to about 18 percent in 2007.

"If you include capital gains like investment and dividend income, the share of the top 1 percent has gone from just over 9 percent to 23.5 percent" (p. 15). The average CEO of the 350 largest companies which were publicly traded "made more than $12 million per year" (Leigh, 2007, as cited in Hacker & Pierson, 2010, p. 62).

Barry (2005) has called this trend the "pathology of inequality" and quotes Morgerson's (2004) data which showed that in 1998 the average CEO compensation was 419 times the pay of the average blue-collar worker, but by 2003 had become 531 times the average. The outrageous salaries of these business leaders have drawn the ire of Congress and even many in the business community, but there is no relief on the horizon (Useem, 2003).

CEOs receive huge salaries and raises even as their businesses tank. At the same time, note Hacker & Pierson (2010), "the economy stopped working for middle-and working-class Americans" (p. 19).

A Conception of Social Justice

We will use the definition of social justice as advanced by John Rawls (1971), that is, social justice is basically *fairness*. And when *fairness* is examined, it has to first be considered outside of the school. An *activist school leader* has not only to understand how the internal mechanisms within a school work against the poor, but how the poor are positioned in the larger social structure before their children ever even arrive in the school. In Rawls' own words,

> The primary subject of justice is the basic structure of society or more exactly, the way in which the major social institutions distribute fundamental rights and duties and determine the division of advantages from social cooperation . . . the major institutions [such as schools] define men's rights and duties and influence their life prospects, what they can expect to be and how well they can hope to do. (p. 7)

A measuring stick for determining the extent of social justice lies on two principles according to Rawls (1971). The first is that "each person is to have an equal right to the most extensive basic liberty compatible with a similar liberty for others," and the second is that "social and economic inequalities are to be arranged so that they are both (a) reasonably expected to be to everyone's advantage, and (b) attached to positions and offices open to all" (p. 60). It is clear from these principles that the very structure of the larger society is part and parcel of a perspective on social justice.

The reality of the situation is that there already exist deep and pervasive socioeconomic inequalities in our society. Those in power with more forms of social and cultural capital exert disproportionate political influence so that their interests are protected at the expense of everyone else. A huge amount of this disproportionate influence and control lies within the business community as underscored by many who know and understand such inequities (Apple, 2006; Emery & Ohanian, 2004; Fraser & Gerstle, 2005; Hacker & Pierson, 2005; 2010; Ravitch, 2010).

As Barry (2005) discusses in his book on social justice, to make a determination of equal opportunity one has to do more than simply open one door at a specific time period and proclaim, "y'all come and apply." Equality has to do with a much earlier time.

The paucity of minority candidates in higher education, for example, or in classroom teaching, is not solved by more intensive recruiting, but rather by making the distribution of education as a critical resource more available to all persons much earlier. And it has to be the kind of education that would enable those who complete it to be considered bona fide applicants.

There is more to this issue as well. For example, Barry indicates that the "socio-economic gap in education has been shown to start as early as 22 months" and that "traditionally, it has widened throughout the education system, culminating in skewed access to higher education" (p. 47). Barry explores how ghetto housing is rife with lead pipes and exposure to arsenic and mercury and that such hazards "caused low birth weight and smaller than normal head circumference both of which have been linked with lower IQ and poor cognitive functioning, such as learning disabilities" (p. 48).

One report cited by Barry is that children exposed to such environmental toxins were "seven times more likely to drop out of school" (Shipler, 2004, p. A15).

The so-called "bottom line" is this. A child's "parents' social class position predicts [their] children's school success and thus their ultimate life chances" (Barry, 2005, p. 15). The opportunity to switch social classes has, according to Barry, "declined in the last twenty years to such a degree that some sociologists have begun to talk about *social closure*" (p. 15).

When Barry (2005) discusses the concept of *social justice*, he means this:

> To put it formally, then: an opportunity to do or obtain something exists for me if there is some course of action lying within my power such that it will lead, if I choose to take it, to my doing or obtaining the thing in question. (p. 20)

The deep structured inequalities which already exist in our society give to some individuals much greater choices than others. For the schools to be solely responsible for making up such inequalities is impossible. They begin years before children ever come to school. True social justice lies beyond schooling. It lies in the larger social structure and the huge disparities which are embedded in it. The *activist school leader*, therefore, understands that schooling is just part of the equation in advancing the cause of *justice as fairness*.

In a discussion of reason and justice in the larger society, Sen (2009) reminds us that it is too easy to attempt to deal with social injustice by simply seeing it at work. Educators see such injustices a good deal of the time as they attempt to educate all of the children coming to them from the larger society. They see abused, malnourished, and poorly clothed children. They see the cumulative shortcomings in student learning and they see discouragement of both the students and the teachers who try to help them.

Yet Sen (2009) says that simply protesting is not enough: "And yet a calamity would be a case of injustice only if it could have been prevented, and particularly if those who could have undertaken preventative action failed to try" (p. 4). Sen advises that avoidance of justification for intervention does "not come from indignant protesters but from placid guardians of order and justice" because those "endowed with public authority . . . are unsure of the grounds for action, or unwilling to scrutinize the basis of their policies" (p. 4).

In presenting a montage of interventions that leaders attempting to turn around failing schools undertake, we see school leaders willing to take the risks of questioning not only themselves, but the policies they are often required to implement and the procedures that accompany them. This includes serious examination of a socioeconomic system that is "built on greed [and which has] incentives for lying, cheating and stealing built into it from the base up" (Barry, 2005, p. 165).

Social Justice within Schools

In chapter 1, table 1.1, we described two views of school performativity. As we have stated, Lens 2 is critical in envisioning education as a public good for all children that promotes social justice in a democratic environment.

We proffer our definition of *social justice* as: schooling which recognizes and respects the fundamental differences in cultural identity and social experiences that place some children and their families at the margins of American culture and society, and which is aimed at removing such barriers which keep them there—not by assimilation (which is social silencing and erasure), but by working to remove the barriers, techniques, beliefs, and practices which put them there in the first place. See chapter 1.

Missing in today's rhetoric of turnaround school practices is the former "good will" known as the public common good. With all aspects of public service under criticism, all public sector services are receiving greater scrutiny. From police and fire departments to teachers, the common, public good has been through the twentieth century protected from management by labor unions.

Today, those unions are under siege. In strained economic times such as these, all public employees are on the chopping block. This present situation requires the *activist school leader* to not only understand what is occurring at a larger scale, but to ensure that *school fairness* is at the heart of how the schooling process is done.

ZOOMING IN ON SCHOOL PERFORMATIVITY

So, what would a turnaround principal need to know and then have the skills, mind, and heart to act upon? Table 5.1 expands on the

Table 5.1. Zooming In on School Performativity

Aspects	Louis, Leithwood, Wahlstrom, & Anderson 2010	• Lens 2 Zoomed In
The Nature of Education		Education is a public service, a social guarantee of an entitlement for all children to promote opportunity, equality and equity. • Continuous community action within the school and broader community of the benefits of public education, i.e., letters to the editor on the successes of students and teachers; articles written for the newspaper to inform the public; hosting coffees and open houses for the public; using the facilities in ways that are meaningful for public use, etc.
The Purpose of Schools	A lack of district support for principals' professional development and sparse contact between principals and their district offices proves problematic.	The purpose of schools is to prepare citizens to function in a democracy that works to progressively expand the benefits of a free society to everyone, especially the most marginalized • District support is critical for effective principals acting purposefully.
The Nature of Leadership	Student achievement is higher in schools where principals share leadership with teachers and the community. Higher-performing schools seek more input from stakeholders on major decisions. Principal turnover has a direct and negative impact on student achievement.	Leadership is a collaborative enterprise to produce greater opportunities to embrace civic humanism and reduce socioeconomic disparities which schools perpetuate. • Collaborative, inclusive leadership is necessary to ensure school leadership ability to turn around underperforming schools. Very effective

Accountability	Districts that emphasize goals and initiatives that extend beyond minimum state expectations have higher levels of student learning.	Accountability is about producing more opportunities to celebrate difference and to become more inclusive, as opposed to exclusive. Tests are only one measure and are not perfect barometers of improved performance • The very nature of school reform efforts that are top-down models requires that turnaround principals understand the philosophical perspective. This will ensure that accountability establishes only the floor and not the ceiling to school reform.
Nature of Management	A lack of district support for principals' professional development and sparse contact between principals and their district offices proves problematic.	The role of management is to expand and differentiate forms of pedagogy and to support creative teaching. • The continued rhetoric of globalization as the main focus for schools denies the common good sensibility. A turnaround principal understands that offering many approaches for students to learn requires teachers skilled in a variety of strategies. A single teacher performance instrument or a data check on student achievement is not to be given more weight over many other aspects of what constitutes success for both the learner and the teacher.
Social Justice		Social justice is a major goal of this view by equalizing opportunity for advancement in the larger society and the role of the school in that society. • We have stressed that for social change to occur social benefits must be expanded and not limited to a one-size-fits-all.

Lens 2 perspective introduced in chapter 1 that we believe is critical to turnaround, socially just, *activist* school leaders.

LEADERSHIP TIED TO STUDENT ACHIEVEMENT

Discussed in the above figure, a recently published five-year study, commissioned by the Wallace Foundation and produced by the Universities of Minnesota and Toronto, "is the largest of its kind to unravel the relationship between school leadership and student achievement" (*NewsLeader*, 2010, September, p. 4). We include it here for its comprehensive research approach.

This study has found high student achievement is directly linked to what they call *collective leadership*, which they define as the sharing of influence in student learning among educators, parents, stakeholders, and community members. The study *Learning from Leadership: Investigating the Links to Improved Student Achievement* drew on a survey of eight thousand teachers and administrators.

The study confirmed school leadership ranks second behind only classroom instruction for influence on student learning. "Essentially, the higher performing the school, the greater the likelihood that more people are dipping their hands into the honey jar of school decisions" (p. 4). This report shows that

> while principals and district leaders still have the most influence on school decisions, they do not lose influence as others gain it. Principals who champion collective leadership and take on *helicopter* roles do not distribute leadership for the sake of reducing their administrative workload. Instead, they are involved in many efforts to improve teaching and learning in addition to their management responsibilities. (p. 4)

This research shows the specific leadership characteristics of principals: confident in their beliefs, actions, and abilities and exhibiting a strong confidence in the collaborative group abilities they foster. The key findings are noted in box 5.1.

Other positive characteristics effective leaders displayed were high respect and trust for teachers, strong support of teacher profes-

---

**BOX 5.1. RELATIONSHIP BETWEEN SCHOOL
LEADERSHIP AND STUDENT ACHIEVEMENT**

- Student achievement is higher in schools where principals share leadership with teachers and the community.
- Higher-performing schools seek more input from stakeholders on major decisions.
- Districts that emphasize goals and initiatives that extend beyond minimum state expectations have higher levels of student learning.
- A lack of district support for principals' professional development and sparse contact between principals and their district offices proves problematic.
- Principal turnover has a direct and negative impact on student achievement. On average, schools experience about one new principal every three to four years. (*NewsLeader*, 2010, p. 4)

---

sional development, and visiting classrooms with a strong focus on instruction.

Lack of district support, fragmented professional development, and ineffective data use were the negatives to effective school leadership. And, according to the report, high principal turnover seemed to do the most damage.

> On average, schools experience about one new principal every three to four years, an event that negatively impacts school culture, the report confirms. On the bright side, that impact is minimized in schools where leadership is distributed among teachers. Shared leadership distribution can moderate the negative consequences of rapid principal turnover, but only where existing school cultures are strong and supportive of teacher leadership, the report said. (*NewsLeader*, 2010, p. 4)

As Rothman (2010) states, "Leaders—all of them—need a new set of skills" (p. 1). To which we add a greater understanding of the human agency and what we have termed the accoutrements of *activist leaders*.

BECOMING THE ACTIVIST LEADER

From the principal-in-training perspective Papa (2011) proposed six features to becoming socially just *activist* leaders that are not usually found in university preparation programs. Papa (2011) has defined as the "accoutrements" of leadership: the perspectives and outlooks concerning leadership developed through application and practice and which are descriptively *sewn* into one's persona as s/he develops into a fully fledged leader.

These accoutrements to leadership will shape the activist leader by attending to both the heart and mind. These are shown in box 5.2.

BOX 5.2. THE PAPA ACCOUTREMENTS OF SOCIALLY JUST *ACTIVIST* LEADERS

Adult Learners

Leaders should know adult learners learn on a need-to-know basis (Papa & Papa, 2011). Teacher professional development must be anchored on adult learning principles. If we know how a learner approaches the acquisition of knowledge then we can arrange strategies that will enhance their learning. Fairness for the adult learner takes the learner at his/her particular learning point.

Human Agency

We know one-size-fits-all does not work. The totality of our students' mental, physical, and spiritual aspects is the package that must be taken into perspective. How better to understand human agency? We must ensure the future school leader has a varied repertoire of fair and just behaviors.

Ignored Intended Skills

How do we measure a good listener? We know it is vital for the socially just *activist* leader to be caring and compassionate. Vision building requires it. Strong personnel relations demand it and have the understanding that it is okay and normal to wrestle with complex issues.

Intellectual Curiosity

A leader is curious. We can prepare school leaders to be curious of their school setting. Curiosity in learning and how it is fostered in the school environment is critical for school staff to develop, understand and apply. Curiosity is fairness in action as it asks "why" with no assigning of blame.

Futurity

Technology gives us a false sense that it should be easier to solve the problems we face within our schools than it really is, while providing supposed efficiencies. And, we now know that when problems become too difficult students can move on to charter or for-profit schools, leaving behind public schools. Leaders must be exposed to learning frames that go against the grain of current wisdom. Going against the grain may just be the best leader trait we can encourage.

Imaginativeness

Creative, inspired, original, resourceful, visionary, artistic, inventive, ingenious are the synonyms to imaginative leadership. Experience with good heart, an almost spiritual need to be of service for others; to be the hope for others; to help others be all they can be; to see the good in others is limited only by one's lack of imagination.

HEURISTICS FOR THE ACTIVIST LEADER

Heuristic 15: Activist educational leaders understand that social justice involves the whole of society and not just the schools. While activist school leaders have primary responsibilities for their schools' operations, they understand that schools are the recipients of students from all classes of society and that some come with many more advantages and with experiences that put them ahead of their classmates—or behind, as the case may be. School as an institution is not a socially neutral place. It is representative of the interests, perspective, outlook, culture, and mores of the dominant elites who control them.

Bourdieu and Passeron (2000) call this "the cultural arbitrary" (p. 16). There are many inequalities in the larger society, and schools in most nations reproduce those inequalities. The activist school leader fully understands this essentially conservative fact and works to create an educational environment which does not reproduce such inequalities.

Heuristic 16: The dominant reform models pushed on schools by the federal and state agencies and many foundations in education are exemplars of machine bureaucracy. Any examination of the features of "reforming schools" today reflects the characteristics of machine bureaucracy. There is the relentless pressure to standardize everything, creating an educational Procrustean bed for teachers and students and dealing with resistance to that model with punishment via merit systems linked to pay according to performance by student test scores on standardized tests. Standardized tests eliminate student individual differences as a calculus in evaluating learning. If such did not erase such differences they could not be called "objective."

Standardized testing assumes all children are the same and if not, they cannot be compared, ranked, or evaluated. As Au (2009) indicates, ". . . standardized testing essentially *commodifies* students, that is, the tests turn students into commodities to be produced, inspected, and compared" (p. 41), while turning teachers into laborers on factory assembly lines. Schools are factories and what is desired are indicators of machine efficiency, i.e., continuous, flawless, and impersonal. When schools become factories they are morally bankrupt.

Heuristic 17: The activist educational leader understands the importance of cultural capital in turning around schools and has no place for deficit metaphors for students.

Schools represent a specific form of cultural capital of various social classes in the larger society. Cultural capital is "a form of value associated with culturally authorized tastes, consumption patterns, attributes, skills and awards" (Webb, Schirato & Danaher, 2002, p. x). Cultural capital varies by social class and much of it is purchased with money and the forms of it can be translated to money through access to the job market.

Educational institutions are those agencies which bestow forms of cultural capital on students in the form of diplomas and degrees. Students from various social classes come to schools with different forms of cultural capital. Those students from social classes which are most congruent with those of the school do much better in them than those who have less or little experience with the approved modes of cultural capital.

The activist educational leader looks at students who have not had access to dominant forms of cultural capital as neither stupid nor deficient, but simply as different. Deficit mental models of students who are different are not compatible with turning around low-performing schools. All students are capable, but they are different. Good instruction will magnify those differences, not reduce them.

Heuristic 18: The activist educational leader is intentional in developing leadership by embracing both the heart and mind. The socially just activist leader must be thoughtful not only with others but with oneself. Skills and management techniques can be learned. How we respect others and provide *fairness* in opportunities for all asks the school leader to delve deeper into one's own heart: to be curious and imaginative when dealing with the current wisdom.

CONCLUSION

Activist educational leaders are unhappy with the status quo, not only with how some schools are failing, but also with the approved antidotes prescribed for them to become better. An experienced school administrator summarized this stance when he wrote:

> It dawned on us that the language of reform was not primarily and centrally about education. Rather, it was about economic ideology, sometimes called the "business agenda"—full of phrases like economic advantage, competition, customer satisfaction, consumers, products, stakeholders, entrepreneurship, human resources, and the like. . . . The words of education reform revealed its purposes, leaving us feeling betrayed. Second, any serious notions of education seemed

absent from the debate—indeed, the discussion sounded to us like the promotion of a kind of economic patriotism . . . our country and its people will lose their "competitive advantage." (Wiens, 2006, p. 216)

Turning around low-performing schools means coming to grips with the question of what the purpose of public schooling is and the linkage between what the schools do and how they enable our society to become more socially just and fair. Confronting the deep inequalities in our larger social structure and how schools perpetuate them is one of the first realizations important to the activist educational leader.

Marable (2002) cites a California education professor who captured our perspective best when she said, "A public school has both internal public purposes and external public purposes. The internal purpose is learning, but the external purpose is to build community" (p. 133).

Explicit Leader Beliefs and Actions

1. Ask the hard questions that guide our craft: Successful leaders know they must walk the community and work to enhance its collectivity in all aspects of the school. Reflection for the school leader means throw the mirror away and encourage feedback to help guide schooling practices.
2. Encourage teachers to become learners again: We believe in school leaders taking and giving feedback to learn what you and your teachers don't know. Understanding adult learners will guide the school leader so that changing the mind-sets of teachers of culturally different kids can occur. Teachers learn from each other, so encourage peer support among them.
3. Sponsor professional development that fosters culturally responsive pedagogy: Successful leaders know how to build collaborations through professional learning communities to ensure cultural competence and excellence. Knowing how to hold courageous conversations around poverty, race, ethnicity, gender, etc., is critical to turning around a school's performance.

Troubleshooting Guide

- It's more than the kids: Low-performing or failing schools are normally comprised of many students from the most marginalized classes in America. Many other nations have similar problems with students from their lower classes (Bernstein, 1996). Avoid "blaming the victims" for not having access to the full panoply of choices of more privileged students from the more well-off classes. Schools are a peculiar form of social agency and its routines and assumptions about the kids.

- Beware of factory models being pushed on you as exemplars: Most of the reform models being advanced by the federal and state governments and many accreditation associations as well as prominent foundations are nothing more than warmed-over versions of Frederick Taylor's scientific management approach. The give-away for them is that they employ a bevy of machine metaphors such as "continuous progress," "data driven decision making," "customers," "competition" and the like.

  Factory models require standardization, identical inputs for identical outputs. And while such approaches have helped construct a worldwide fast-food industry along the lines of Burger King, McDonald's, and Taco Bell, students cannot be standardized, and because they can't be standardized neither can the curriculum, the classes, the books, nor the educational experience.

- Leadership is not about punishing one's way to excellence: A huge amount of the push to "cure" low-performing schools is represented in a wide range of punishments. Connecting teacher and administrator pay to student performance on standardized tests is not only punishment, it is a form of organization control. In the bestselling book by Eric Schlosser (2001) called *Fast Food Nation* he wrote, "The strict regimentation at fast food restaurants creates standardized products. It increases throughput. And it gives fast food companies an enormous power over their employees. . . . The management no longer depends upon the talents or skills of its workers— those things are built into the operating system and machines. Jobs that have been 'deskilled' can be filled cheaply. The need to retain any individual worker is greatly reduced by the ease with which he or she can be replaced" (p. 70).

No teacher wants to fail and no teacher wants to work in a failing school. Punishing them is not the way to create community nor is their resistance to becoming an assembly line worker unhealthy. The problem with low-performing schools is not controlling them more minutely, but creating in them a place where teaching and learning (as opposed to testing) are honored, promoted, and rewarded.

REFERENCES

Apple, M. (2006). *Educating the "right" way: Markets, standards, God, and inequality.* New York: Routledge.

Au, W. (2009). *Unequal by design: High-stakes testing and the standardization of inequality.* New York: Routledge.

Barry, B. (2005). *Why social justice matters.* Malden, MA: Polity Press.

Bernstein, B. (1996). *Pedagogy, symbolic control and identity: Theory, research, critique.* London: Taylor & Francis.

Bourdieu, P., & Passeron, J. C. (2000). *Reproduction in education, society and culture,* 2nd ed. London: Sage.

The Economist (2006, June 17). The rich, the poor and the growing gap between them—Inequality in America, 379 (8482), pp. 28–30).

Emery, K., & Ohanian, S. (2004). *Why is corporate America bashing our public schools?* Portsmouth, NH: Heinemann.

Fraser, S., & Gerstle, G. (2005). *Ruling America: A history of wealth and power in a democracy.* Cambridge, MA: Harvard University Press.

Hacker, J., & Pierson, P. (2005). *Off center: The Republican revolution and the erosion of American democracy.* New Haven, CT: Yale University Press.

Hacker, J., & Pierson, P. (2010). *Winner-take-all politics: How Washington made the rich richer—and turned its back on the middle class.* New York: Simon & Schuster.

Iyer, R. (1973). *The moral and political thought of Mahatma Gandhi.* New York: Oxford University Press.

Kanigel, R. (1997). *The one best way: Frederick Winslow Taylor and the enigma of efficiency.* New York: Viking.

Lawrence-Lightfoot, S. (1983). *The good high school: Portraits of character and culture.* New York: Basic Books, Inc.

Leigh, A. (2007, November). How closely do income shares track other measures of inequality? *Economic Journal* 117: 589–603.

Louis, K. S., Leithwood, K., Wahlstrom, K. L., & Anderson, S. E. (2010). Learning from leadership: Investigating the links to improved student learning. *Final Report of Research to the Wallace Foundation.* St. Paul, MN: University of Minnesota.

Lumby, J., & English, F. (2010). *Leadership as lunacy: And other metaphors for educational leadership.* Thousand Oaks, CA: Corwin Press.

Marable, M. (2002). *The great wells of democracy: The meaning of race in American life.* New York: Basic Books, Inc.

Mintzberg, H. (1983). *Structure in fives: Designing effective organizations.* Englewood Cliffs, NJ: Prentice-Hall, Inc.

Morgerson, G. (2004, January 25). Explaining (or not) why the boss is paid so much. *New York Times*, Section 3, p. 1.

NewsLeader. (2010, September). Best principals espouse collective leadership, research finds. *NewsLeader*, 58 (1), p. 4.

Papa, R. (2011). Standards for educational leaders: Promises, paradoxes and pitfalls. In F. English (ed.), *Sage handbook of educational leadership,* 2nd ed. Thousand Oaks, CA: Sage Publications.

Papa [aka Papa-Lewis], R., & Fortune, R. (2002). *Leadership on purpose: Promising practices for African American and Hispanic students.* Thousand Oaks, CA: Corwin.

Papa, R., & Papa, J. (2011). Leading adult learners: Preparing future leaders and professional development of those they lead. In R. Papa (ed.), *Technology leadership for school improvement.* Thousand Oaks, CA: Sage Publications.

Ravitch, D. (2010). *The death and life of the great American school system: How testing and choice are undermining education.* New York: Perseus Books.

Rawls, J. (1971). *A theory of justice.* Cambridge, MA: Harvard University Press.

Rhee, M. (2011, January 11). In budget crises, an opening for school reform. *The Wall Street Journal*, A17.

Rothman, R. (2010). *Leadership in smart systems.* Retrieved October 5, 2010, from http://www.annenberginstitute.org/VUE/leadership-in-smart-systems.

Schlosser, E. (2001). *Fast food nation: The dark side of the All-American meal.* Boston: Houghton Mifflin Company.

Sen, A. (2009). *The idea of justice.* Cambridge, MA: Harvard University Press.

Shipler, D. (2004, February 12). Total poverty awareness. *New York Times,* A15.

Sparks, S. (2011, January 12). Are bad schools immortal? The scarcity of turnarounds and shutdowns in both charter and district sectors. *Education Week,* 30 (15), 5.

Useem, J. (2003, April 28). Have they no shame? *Fortune,* pp. 56–58.

Virshup, A. (2011, January 16). Anatomy of a school crisis: A student's drowning and a principal's firing reveal divisions at an academy in Harlem. *The New York Times,* p. 27.

Webb, J., Schirato, T. & Danaher, G. (2002). *Understanding Bourdieu.* London: Sage.

Wiens, J. (2006). Educational leadership as civic humanism. In P. Kellher and R. Van Der Bogert (eds.), *Voices for democracy: Struggles and celebrations of transforming leaders* (pp. 199–225). Malden, MA: Blackwell.

Wise, A. (1979). *Legislated learning: The bureaucratization of the American classroom.* Berkeley, CA: University of California Press.

Appendix A

HEURISTICS FOR THE ACTIVIST LEADER

CHAPTER 1

Heuristic 1: A dramatic change should be signaled (low evidence).

The data from the WWC indicated that there has to be a signal of some sort that things are not going to be same as before, an important sign to those inside and outside the school that a significant break or interruption is going to occur. What this means is that awareness has to be created that it's not going to be "business as usual" any longer. There is no one "best way" to signal such a change. The means should fit the context however. And the "fit" is not a matter of science, but one of "art."

Heuristic 2: A consistent focus on instruction (low evidence).

The key to turning around a low-performing school is to focus on instruction. The reason is not hard to discern. Student performance is normally determined by test scores because they are the cheapest means to define performance. One must know how "low performance" is defined before attempting to organize the energies of the people inside and outside of a school site. Differentiating instruction and making sure it is aligned to the means of measurement is usually a key element in engaging in "improvement" (English, 2010).

Heuristic 3: Select improvements that are visible and easiest to secure (low evidence).

There are many means to securing school improvement. Heuristic 2 indicated that they should be focused on instruction. This heuristic requires the school leader and staff to sort through and make those improvements which have the best chance of making an impact very early in the process.

Early wins provide confidence both to those inside the school and to constituents and even critics that better times are on the way. To do this requires some sophistication in understanding what the factors and variables are in supporting the entire instructional/curricula process.

Simplistic business models are usually ignorant of the core of the educational enterprise. Business models are about management and not about instruction, except perhaps to search for ways to reduce costs and improve efficiencies. It is possible to have a well-managed school and low student achievement. One does not usually imply the other. However, if a school is poorly managed overall, that usually includes the instructional program and hence the appearance is that if managerial techniques are installed to create order, this will somehow improve instructional performance as well.

Heuristic 4: Build a committed staff (low evidence).

The key to leadership in turning low-performing schools around is that there has to be a "critical mass" of like-minded professionals and support staff who are committed to improvement. While we think that the word "culture" is often overused for schools—as is "climate"—there has to be a concerted effort to create a sense of palpable expectations for change which requires concerted work toward change and toward advancement. The school leader works *with and through people*.

The ability of the principal to connect with and excite teachers and staff and convince mostly by example is pivotal in school improvement. The principal has to be "out front" but can't be the only one "in front." Finding ways for many people to shine is a key. The old saying, "It's amazing how much can be accomplished if one is not worried about who gets the credit" epitomizes the posture of the school leader.

CHAPTER 2

Heuristic 5: Educational reform is complex, multifaceted, and interactive.

There have been many attempts at educational reform in the U.S. over a two-hundred-year period. While some were initially successful, none have been able to be sustained except the graded school which is one of the few exceptions to sustainability. However, the graded school carries enormous educational baggage and continues to be a major barrier to breaking what Sarason (1990) has called "the encapsulated classroom" (p. 111) tradition.

Educational reform cannot be considered an approach involving a simple checklist which is enacted upon stable organizational entities. Schools are dynamic and fluid despite how they may appear to outsiders. Any reform that attempts to change internal dynamics must be considered interactional and not static. Schools are living organisms and changes that are "successful" in one context may not be so in another because the internal dynamics and relationships vary from site to site.

Heuristic 6: The motivations and goals of educational reformers are not the same.

Any study of the history of the reformers of education in the U.S. will show that some were prompted by altruistic goals of educating the masses while others were looking for cheap and quick educational fixes. Many reformers are still looking for quick fixes and too many believe that the corporate model of "one size fits all" and top-down change will reform the schools so that they work for everyone and not simply the well-to-do. In this they are mistaken.

Reformers do not all agree on what constitutes a reform. Many reforms are profoundly anti-democratic. While the rhetoric about changing schools is usually about students and learning, many reforms have little or anything to do with learning at all. Rather they are about imposing a "for-profit" mind-set on the schools where the major beneficiaries are not students at all, but the owners and stockholders.

Heuristic 7: Many reforms have little to do with social justice.

Many educational reforms propose changes that have little to do with altering the socioeconomic-political status quo. Schools continue to act as conservative social agents that reproduce the culture and status of those in control of the country and its economic agents. Some reforms benefit those who are now in control of the schools and enhance their position. Not everyone benefits from reforming schools. It all depends on who is defining the reform and what is the content of it.

CHAPTER 3

Heuristic 8: The public school pupil mix will continue to be even more diverse than it is today, calling into question the existing dominance of the Euro-American majoritarian cultural perspective on many fronts, from "core curriculums" to "standardized tests."

All of the demographic trends concerning the racial and ethnic composition of the U.S. indicate the country is becoming more and more diverse. In fact, it is estimated that by the year 2050 whites will no longer be the majority. The largest gain will be from Hispanics and minority children will become the majority by 2031 (Yen, 2009).

For years minority children have been at a disadvantage when they are immersed in a school culture that is alien and often incommensurable with their lived life experiences. Their lack of success in schools is due to this disadvantage as they drop out in larger numbers and as their alienation grows (MacLeod, 1987; Solomon, 1992).

Increasingly, the tension between the cultural perspectives of the once dominant majority Euro-American view will be called into question as to its propriety and relevance. For example, Au (2009) has indicated that standardized tests institutionalize inequality because it is a statistical impossibility for all students to reach 100 percent proficiency because standardized tests "require that a certain percentage of students fail in order to be considered valid and reliable" (Popham, 2001, as cited in Au, 2009, p. 138). Gibson (2001) has called high stakes testing "a form of regulated elitism" (as cited in Au, 2009, p. 139).

Heuristic 9: The profound quandary of African-American and Native American students in schools dominated by Euro-American cultural perspectives places them at extreme risk of alienation and failure.

The dominant cultural perspective outlined by Boykin (1986) in this chapter places some minority students at an extreme disadvantage in the schools. An activist leader works to create awareness on the part of the faculty and support staff of this fundamental problem and works to ease the tensions involved.

One solution is to teach both cultures in the school and to make majoritarian students aware of their own cultural lenses in the process. An activist leader also works to create understanding that the curriculum is biased if it does not question the cultural arbitrary embedded within it, and so are tests and other educational materials and accompanying pedagogies if they are not interrogated as well.

Heuristic 10: Poverty is not a random variable among children and the inequality gap is growing in the U.S.

The large repository of research and statistics continues to demonstrate that poverty does not embrace American school children as a random (or chance) variable. Rather, poverty impacts Americans disproportionately, that is, concentrating on African American, Native American, and Hispanic student populations in very great numbers.

Research shows that it is far more difficult for black families to remove themselves from poverty than white families (Hertz, 2005). Black families are much more likely to remain poor over several generations than white families. The income gap in the United States between rich and poor is expanding. It is the second highest of all countries in the world, behind only China (*The Economist*, 2011). This trend is profoundly troubling for the future of a democracy.

CHAPTER 4

Heuristic 11: School leadership success is intimately connected to school district leadership success.

While it may be convenient and even romantic to think about turning schools around in isolation, an individual principal and his/her faculty can only do so much in isolation. S/he will require increased resource support, perhaps some waivers from larger school system policies, regulations, and practices, and strong political support when the times get rough as they inevitably will (Duke & Jacobson, 2011).

The commitment of the central office to their low-performing schools has to be manifest in "a commitment by the board and the superintendent to work together collaboratively, to candidly assess the strengths and weaknesses of the district, to put aside issues which do not impact achievement and to build community support for their plans" (Snipes, Doolittle & Herlihy, 2002, p. 63). There is an increasing awareness that superintendent stability is one of the cornerstones of success in turning schools around.

Heuristic 12: District leaders must face down pressures to treat all the schools the same in spite of their performance.

There are enormous pressures on school district leaders to treat all the schools the same. Making exceptions without the buffer of a federal or state law for various exceptionalities is politically dangerous. When more funds flow to schools serving children from the lower classes, the politically powerful elites who normally exercise control may exert resistance and a backlash occurs. There can be an expressed fear that somehow if "those children" succeed "our children" will not enjoy the cultural and educational advantages to which they are *entitled*.

Despite the rhetoric to the contrary, not everyone wants all children to do well in the schools, especially if it means that limited resources are redirected to those perceived not to be the same or *deserving*. It takes great courage for district leaders to confront these forces and pressures and often boards are representative of those class-centered interests.

Heuristic 13: The creation of an effectively aligned curriculum within a centralized testing program is a school district responsibility, while differentiated instruction is a school site responsibility.

The key to improving scores on standardized tests of accountability rests on curriculum alignment (English, 2010) and differentiated instruction (Thousand, Villa & Nevin, 2007). While curriculum alignment is a central responsibility, differentiated instruction is a school unit responsibility (Ward, 2004, p. 10).

Schools and school district personnel must share in the blame and/or the success of their efforts. If the curriculum to be tested is not taught, it doesn't matter if instruction is differentiated. However, if an aligned curriculum is not taught well and differentiated by critical differences in learners and learning styles, it will similarly not be as effective as it might be otherwise.

Heuristic 14: While school leadership involves learning, it is actually acquired (i.e., *an act of accoutering*) through development and practice.

The "accoutrements" of leadership are not simply discrete skills, though some skills are part of being accoutered. The word *accoutrement* was borrowed from Middle French in 1596 and is traced back to the Renaissance Latin "accosturare" which meant to arrange or to sew something (Barnhart, 1995, p. 6). In contemporary terms it means an article of equipment or dress which is acquired. Used in the research performed for this book, it refers to perspectives and outlooks concerning leadership developed through application and practice and which are descriptively *sewn* into one's persona as s/he develops into a fully fledged leader.

We fully believe leaders are made and not born. They develop and learn, make mistakes, and continue developing. We don't believe in traits because that would connote some sort of genetic origination. Leaders come to leadership and develop themselves. In the words of Warren Bennis (1989), "Leaders have nothing but themselves to work with" (p. 47).

CHAPTER 5

Heuristic 15: Activist educational leaders understand that social justice involves the whole of society and not just the schools.

While activist school leaders have primary responsibilities for their schools' operations, they understand that schools are the recipients of students from all classes of society and that some come with many more advantages and with experiences that put them ahead of their classmates—or behind, as the case may be. School as an institution is not a socially neutral place. It is representative of the interests, perspective, outlook, culture, and mores of the dominant elites who control them.

Bourdieu and Passeron (2000) call this "the cultural arbitrary" (p. 16). There are many inequalities in the larger society, and schools in most nations reproduce those inequalities. The activist school leader fully understands this essentially conservative fact and works to create an educational environment which does not reproduce such inequalities.

Heuristic 16: The dominant reform models pushed on schools by the federal and state agencies and many foundations in education are exemplars of machine bureaucracy.

Any examination of the features of "reforming schools" today reflects the characteristics of machine bureaucracy. There is the relentless pressure to standardize everything, creating an educational Procrustean bed for teachers and students and dealing with resistance to that model with punishment via merit systems linked to pay according to performance by student test scores on standardized tests. Standardized tests eliminate student individual differences as a calculus in evaluating learning. If such did not erase such differences they could not be called "objective."

Standardized testing assumes all children are the same and if not, they cannot be compared, ranked, or evaluated. As Au (2009) indicates, ". . . standardized testing essentially *commodifies* students, that is, the tests turn students into commodities to be produced, inspected, and compared" (p. 41), while turning teachers into laborers on factory assembly lines. Schools are factories and what is desired are indicators of machine efficiency, i.e., continuous, flawless, and impersonal. When schools become factories they are morally bankrupt.

Heuristic 17: The activist educational leader understands the importance of cultural capital in turning around schools and has no place for deficit metaphors for students.

Schools represent a specific form of cultural capital of various social classes in the larger society. Cultural capital is "a form of value associated with culturally authorized tastes, consumption patterns, attributes, skills and awards" (Webb, Schirato & Danaher, 2002, p. x). Cultural capital varies by social class and much of it is purchased with money and the forms of it can be translated to money through access to the job market.

Educational institutions are those agencies which bestow forms of cultural capital on students in the form of diplomas and degrees. Students from various social classes come to schools with different forms of cultural capital. Those students from social classes which are most congruent with those of the school do much better in them than those who have less or little experience with the approved modes of cultural capital.

The activist educational leader looks at students who have not had access to dominant forms of cultural capital as neither stupid nor deficient, but simply as different. Deficit mental models of students who are different are not compatible with turning around low-performing schools. All students are capable, but they are different. Good instruction will magnify those differences, not reduce them.

Heuristic 18: The activist educational leader is intentional in developing their leadership by embracing both the heart and mind.

The socially just activist leader must be thoughtful not only with others but with oneself. Skills and management techniques can be learned. How we respect others and provide *fairness* in opportunities for all asks the school leader to delve deeper into one's own heart: to be curious and imaginative when dealing with the current wisdom.

Appendix B

EXPLICIT LEADER BELIEFS AND ACTIONS

CHAPTER 1

1. **A refusal to accept the status quo as inevitable:** We believe our observations and data support the assertion that successful leaders of turnaround schools refuse to accept the status quo. They refuse to engage in actions which perpetuate a culture of low expectations and the inevitability of a permanent underclass based on race and class in America. While they don't deny it exists, they deny it is inevitable and certainly deny it is a sign of a healthy and democratic political system or bodes well for its future.

2. **A refusal to accept low-performing or failing schools as permanent features of public education:** Successful leaders of turnaround or failing schools do not accept them as permanent features of public education. They see them as social constructs and therefore as changeable. Making them successful means understanding how success is defined and

how to relate the workings and complex interactions within such schools to become successful. While they are respectful of humans working in such schools, they are relentless (not ruthless) in working toward consensus of the need for change; connecting actions to that change and working toward higher levels of success. They do not believe that low-performing or failing schools represent having to educate "inferior" students.

3. **A commitment to social justice and schools as levers of social change:** Successful leaders of turnaround or failing schools envision them as levers of social change, if nothing more than enabling the students to escape the "blame the victim" mentality that is part and parcel of neo-liberalism and the ideology of school choice that in the words of Brian Barry (2007) "hold(s) poor people responsible for choices that arise directly from the relatively limited set of options that poverty (by definition) gives rise to in the market" (p. 87).

CHAPTER 2

1. **A commitment to a participatory process:** We believe our observations and data support the assertion that successful leaders of turnaround schools lead by inclusive styles. The participation of all "players" in the design and execution of the change processes is critical for the success of the reform.

2. **A commitment to understanding who is doing the speaking:** Successful leaders of turnaround or failing schools do not accept such labels as permanent features of public education that serve as poorly disguised benchmarks. Knowing where the reform agenda is philosophically based pushes the school

leader to ensure that labels serve little purpose in the process of "very effective" school processes.

3. **A commitment to social justice:** As we have said, school reform is not for the faint of heart. The school-societal nexus remains the flashpoint for social reform and the tackling of the larger societal inequities and inequalities.

CHAPTER 3

1. **Respect and understand family, home, and the cultures of your students:** Leaders fundamentally respect the cultural backgrounds of their students and parents as not deficient but distinctive. The public schools exist to serve and educate all the children of all the people. Understand that the more a specific culture is aligned with the Euro-American culture the more likely students will experience success, and the more students' lived cultural experiences are at odds with that culture, the more likely their success becomes problematic.

2. **Some forms of student resistance to the school are a healthy sign of their protest, their desire not to be erased or have their cultural identities compromised:** In a school where minority students perceive the school as being skewed toward white students, their opposition and resistance to the school can be associated with a desire to avoid having their distinctiveness erased (Fordham & Ogbu, 1986). Similarly, the creation and maintenance of a separate black cultural identity required African-American students to oppose school norms and to take out their frustrations on fellow minority students who did conform because they were "acting white" (Solomon, 1992, p. 4).

School leaders must create a student climate that does not require cultural identities to be erased in order for minority students to do well in schools. Student solidarity around cultural identities is required by them for survival "in a hostile, urban, street corner environment" (Solomon, 1992, p. 4). Punishing students for trying to survive in the world they live in is counterproductive.

CHAPTER 4

1. **Your persona matters:** Understand that you must continually throughout your career reflect and examine who you are. How you practice your craft reflects what your perspectives and outlook is *sewn* into your persona.
2. **Remain intellectually curious and imaginative:** Going against the grain is only possible if you remain curious and can imagine a better school practice. What little one can control from outside sources is countered in one's enormous capacity to rethink, refocus and reflect on how to make a difference in students' lives.

CHAPTER 5

1. **Ask the hard questions that guide our craft:** Successful leaders know they must walk the community and work to enhance its collectivity in all aspects of the school. Reflection for the school leader means throw the mirror away and encourage feedback to help guide schooling practices.
2. **Encourage teachers to become learners again:** We believe in school leaders taking and giving feedback to learn what you and your teachers don't know. Understanding adult learners will guide the school leader so that changing the mind-sets of teachers of culturally different kids can occur. Teachers learn from each other, so encourage peer support among them.

3. **Sponsor professional development that fosters culturally responsive pedagogy:** Successful leaders know how to build collaborations through professional learning communities to ensure cultural competence and excellence. Knowing how to hold courageous conversations around poverty, race, ethnicity, gender, and so on, is critical to turning around a school's performance.

Appendix C

TROUBLESHOOTING GUIDE

CHAPTER 1

- **No single thing will solve all the problems:** Because low-performing or failing schools are complex combinations of interactions and responses, low performance or failure is not the result of any single action or reaction. Rather it is the sum of a series of actions (or lack thereof) and reactions over an extended period of time. Our research shows that schools cannot be turned around on a dime, that lasting change takes many years and may extend over the tenure of more than one leader. No single change, intervention, or innovation will magically turn schools around. Do not search for "quick fixes," as there are none. Look for combinations of things which have to occur simultaneously and sometimes sequentially.
- **All constituents must be involved:** While the most important group to be involved in school changes are teachers, their input and support will not be enough to carry the day. Parental

and student understanding of what is going to be changed and why also are critical features. Develop a comprehensive strategy that involves all the stakeholders in a conversation about change.

- **Your commitment must be transparent:** The leader's commitment to turning a school around is displayed in every possible situation, and no occasion is too small or unimportant to build commitments and create coalitions to transform the school.

CHAPTER 2

- **Concentrate on context:** Beware of checklists which indicate explicitly or implicitly that if the items on the list are all marked off, reform success will always be the result. Context is the key to successful reform. It is rarely 100 percent the same and the actors and interactions are almost always different. So understand what is different about your context from others. What are the unique facets of your students, teachers, parents and your community? How do they interact and come together?
- **Address teaching and learning issues to close educational gaps:** Sarason's (1990; 1993; 1998; 2002; 2004) work shows that without addressing the traditional ideas of teaching and learning in schools, not much will change in them. Schools will continue to perpetuate the socioeconomic status quo. Reformers who want only to impose a new model of governance will only, perhaps, resolve governance issues, whatever they may be. Ask what kinds or reform will reform what? Sarason (2004) said it best: "Teaching is not a science; it is an art fusing ideas, obligations, the personal and interpersonal. The chemistry of that fusion determines whether or how subject matter matters to the students" (p. 199).

CHAPTER 3

- **Single programs will not turn around schools:** A comprehensive approach, one that is culturally sensitive with all constituents is required to ensure the particular programs chosen make sense for the students and community and reduce the feeling of alienation that some student subgroups feel toward an institution which devalues them and their cultural identities.
- **School culture is not neutral and favors some student groups over others in profound and totalizing ways:** School culture, comprised of curriculum content, dominant pedagogy, assumptions about learning and the accepted cultural world view which lies behind all of them including teacher attitudes about students themselves, has to be unlocked carefully and with an eye to breaking the interconnecting parts so that when one's practice or belief is abandoned, it is not replaced with a corollary value or practice which is simply a new name for the old one.
- **Student resistance to school culture and ways is an acquired (learned) response:** Students do not initially come to school hating it. Learning that school is not a place for them or is inhospitable or indifferent to them and their background or potentialities puts students off and over time molds some of them into a defensive, negative, and hostile frame of mind. Turning around schools means taking on beliefs and practices that demean and devalue students. In order to do this successfully, activist leaders must become aware of how schools really work to disenfranchise some students and advantage others.

CHAPTER 4

- **Connect failing schools to failures of the school system:** Most failing schools, especially in urban school districts, are part of a school system. Such schools should not be treated as though they were simply a bad apple in the barrel. In this case, one has to look at the barrel that contains the apples.

A failing school is a school system failure for the simple reason that the control of resources, the provision of selecting competent leaders and teachers, aligning a curriculum to the extant assessment system, is a school system responsibility. What is a local school's responsibility is how the resources are applied and the extent to which instruction is successfully differentiated.

- **Leadership is an acquired mantle which is sewn together from past experiences:** The notion of leadership "accoutrements" is a blend between acquired habits learned through experience, and some habits of mind which are also acquired such as intellectual curiosity and imaginativeness. Educational leaders traffic in a base of moral values because the content of schooling represents an arbitrary choice of many possible "cultures." What supports that base is the dominant value system of the political elites who control schooling in any given culture (Bourdieu & Passeron, 2000). Part of the issue with low-performing schools is that typically the students they are supposed to be educating are from those segments of society who are not from the dominant elite culture. They are at an immediate and continuing disadvantage in a curriculum that is tightly aligned with elite knowledge, language, and cultural capital. To change schooling so that it does something different will require a "metanoia," that is, "a mental revolution, a transformation of one's whole vision of the social world" or at least a new "gaze" (Bourdieu & Wacquant, 1992: as cited in Bolton, 2011, p. 223).

CHAPTER 5

- **It's more than the kids:** Low-performing or failing schools are normally comprised of many students from the most marginalized classes in America. Many other nations have similar problems with students from their lower classes (Bernstein, 1996). Avoid "blaming the victims" for not having access to the full panoply of choices of more privileged students from the more well-off classes. Schools are a peculiar form of social agency and its routines and assumptions about the kids.

- **Beware of factory models being pushed on you as exemplars:** Most of the reform models being advanced by the federal and state governments and many accreditation associations as well as prominent foundations are nothing more than warmed-over versions of Frederick Taylor's scientific management approach. The give-away for them is that they employ a bevy of machine metaphors such as "continuous progress," "data driven decision making," "customers," "competition" and the like.

  Factory models require standardization, identical inputs for identical outputs. And while such approaches have helped construct a worldwide fast-food industry along the lines of Burger King, McDonald's, and Taco Bell, students cannot be standardized, and because they can't be standardized neither can the curriculum, the classes, the books, nor the educational experience.

- **Leadership is not about punishing one's way to excellence:** A huge amount of the push to "cure" low-performing schools is represented in a wide range of punishments. Connecting teacher and administrator pay to student performance on standardized tests is not only punishment, it is a form of organization control. In the bestselling book by Eric Schlosser (2001) called *Fast Food Nation* he wrote, "The strict regimentation at fast food restaurants creates standardized products. It increases throughput. And it gives fast food companies an enormous power over their employees. . . . The management no longer depends upon the talents or skills of its workers—those things are built into the operating system and machines. Jobs that have been 'deskilled' can be filled cheaply. The need to retain any individual worker is greatly reduced by the ease with which he or she can be replaced" (p. 70).

INDEX